USING PEER TUTORING TO IMPROVE READING SKILLS

Using Peer Tutoring to Improve Reading Skills is a very practical guide, offering a straightforward framework and easy-to-implement strategies to help teachers help pupils progress in reading. As a succinct introduction, it shows how schools can make positive use of differences between pupils and turn them into effective learning opportunities.

By outlining the evidence base supporting peer tutoring approaches, it explores the components of the reading process and explains how peer tutoring can be used with any method of teaching reading. Core topics covered include:

- planning and implementing peer tutoring
- getting your school on board
- how to structure effective interaction
- training peer tutors and tutees
- *Paired Reading*—cross-ability approaches
- *One Book for Two*—fostering fluency, reading comprehension and motivation
- *Reading in Pairs*—cross- and same-year tutoring
- supporting struggling readers
- involving families in peer tutoring
- evaluation and feedback.

Illustrated throughout with practical examples from diverse schools across Europe, *Using Peer Tutoring to Improve Reading Skills* is an essential introduction offering easy-to-use guidelines that will support teachers in primary and secondary schools as they enhance pupil motivation and improve reading standards.

Keith Topping is Professor of Educational and Social Research in the School of Education at the University of Dundee, UK, where he is Director of the Centre for Peer Learning.

David Duran is Assistant Professor of Educational Psychology in the Faculty of Sciences of Education at Universitat Autònoma de Barcelona, Spain.

Hilde Van Keer is Professor in the Department of Educational Studies at Ghent University, Belgium.

USING PEER TUTORING TO IMPROVE READING SKILLS

A practical guide for teachers

Keith Topping, David Duran and Hilde Van Keer

Routledge
Taylor & Francis Group

LONDON AND NEW YORK

First published 2016
by Routledge
2 Park Square, Milton Park, Abingdon, Oxon OX14 4RN

and by Routledge
711 Third Avenue, New York, NY 10017

Routledge is an imprint of the Taylor & Francis Group, an informa business

British Library Cataloguing in Publication Data
A catalogue record for this book is available from the British Library

Library of Congress Cataloging in Publication Data
Topping, Keith J.
Using peer tutoring to improve reading skills : a practical guide for teachers /
Keith Topping, David Duran and Hilde Van Keer.
pages cm
1. Reading—Remedial teaching—United States. 2. Peer teaching. 3. Tutors
and tutoring. I. Duran, David. II. Van Keer, Hilde. III. Title.
LB1050.5.T65 2015
372.43—dc23
2015016944

ISBN: 978-1-138-84328-8 (hbk)
ISBN: 978-1-138-84329-5 (pbk)
ISBN: 978-1-315-73103-2 (ebk)

Typeset in Times New Roman
by Swales & Willis Ltd, Exeter, Devon, UK
Printed in Great Britain by Ashford Colour Press Ltd,
Gosport, Hants

CONTENTS

CONTENTS ■ ■ ■ ■

FIGURES

TABLES

FOREWORD

HOW TO USE THIS BOOK

This book is divided into three parts: Introduction, Evidence-based Good Practices and Organising and Implementing Peer Tutoring.

The Introduction has three chapters: the first introduces the stages and background to reading, which is likely to be familiar territory for most readers; the next chapter introduces peer tutoring in general, which may be less familiar to some readers; and the third chapter focuses on the main topic of this book—peer tutoring in reading—and introduces some more challenging concepts.

The second part has six chapters, which report three evidence-based good practices: *Paired Reading*, *One Book for Two* and *Reading in Pairs*. Each method has an initial chapter which describes the practice, followed by a chapter that briefly summarises the background empirical evidence, which will be more demanding to follow.

The third part deals with the practicalities of organising and implementing peer tutoring and covers Chapters 10 to 14. Generally, these chapters are not difficult to follow. Chapters 10 and 11 are concerned with making peer tutoring work, first by careful planning and second by careful implementation. The following chapter reconsiders the role of the teacher in peer tutoring, since this is likely to change from standard expectations (but will be no less busy!). Then, ways of evaluating peer tutoring are outlined—this chapter may require more concentration. Remember, you need to think of evaluation when you are planning your project—do not just try to attach it at the end! Finally, the important issue of sustaining and embedding peer tutoring is discussed—obviously, this is not necessary until you have implemented some peer tutoring projects, but will be of great importance later if peer tutoring is to survive should you decide to leave your school.

The eResources website that accompanies this book is available at: www.routledge.com/9781138843295. Here you will find many practical tools to help you implement your peer tutoring in reading projects. Each item can easily be downloaded for use in the classroom and can be used as it is, or customised by you to suit your local needs.

PART

I

INTRODUCTION

1 READING

Language is the most important skill for children to have mastered if they are to succeed in the school system—and indeed, for later employment and to function as active members of the knowledge society. The version of language that we most often see in the school curriculum is reading—the unlocking of the language in a written text so that it is accessible and open to interpretation, debate and question. Being successful at reading is closely related to competence with language; being successful at reading is the key to unlocking every kind of written text in every subject the student will encounter in school. Consequently, reading is very highly correlated with overall school achievement (Organisation for Economic Co-operation and Development (OECD), 2009).

Learning to read goes through developmental stages as the child grows older. At the *preschool stage*, the amount of talk the parents have with their child is crucial in developing the child's language—and in particular, the number of conversational turns they have with their child. The quality of parent–child interaction can vary, from simple and repetitive language, to the parent modelling more complex and elaborative language which the child copies. When parents read books to their preschool children, more unusual words and sentences are used than in ordinary conversation and the session goes on for longer. So reading to children (even if they do not fully understand it) develops language as well as the other way round (Gilkerson, Richards & Topping, forthcoming).

At *primary/elementary school*, children are assumed to be able to use language and the emphasis is on teaching reading. In the US in particular there has been debate about the 'best' way of teaching reading at this level. Some suggest that teaching 'phonology' (or decoding) is the best way; others that a 'sight word' approach involving emphasis on remembering individual items of vocabulary is best; and yet others suggest that a 'whole language' approach involving reading continuous meaningful text and extracting comprehension is best.

One problem with the phonological approach is that half of the words in the English language (for instance) are not phonologically regular and cannot be attacked by this method. With the sight word approach though, there is the potential problem that it can leave children unable to read any word they have not previously encountered and studied—unless of course children automatically extract some of the rules for attacking new words from their past experiences. And in the whole language approach, if children are not already familiar with the words involved, they are not likely to be able to read the text flowingly, and might tend to focus on texts which offer them little challenge. In fact, most teachers are fully aware that all of these elements need to be part of a comprehensive reading teaching programme. In all cases, the reader plays an active role in building the meaning of the text through their previous knowledge, abilities and motivation (Aarnoutse & Schellings, 2003).

Different components of the reading process can be identified. Early on there may be some emphasis on accuracy—the ability to read each word out loud correctly. Of course, this is merely the first step to the next stage of understanding the meaning of the word—comprehension—and using it in conversation and writing. Once some comprehension is established, teachers can become interested in fluency—the ability of the child to read and understand words in a smooth continuous flow and to articulate them with expression. These components, of course, have a strong interdependent relationship and none of them can be developed without the others. However, because we read to understand the meaning, reading comprehension is seen as being at the core of reading, especially in schools.

Once children move up to *secondary* or *high school*, the emphasis shifts again. Whereas primary school was about learning to read, secondary school is more about reading to learn. Consequently, there is typically less emphasis on the teaching of reading—the assumption being that children have learned how to do this in primary school. Secondary teachers are subject specialists and those subjects do not include reading. But paradoxically, the requirement for reading comprehension ability becomes progressively higher, as texts become more complex. This fact means that the need to develop and improve reading comprehension is not finished and therefore strategies for this have to be taught.

While children are in secondary/high school, the amount of reading they are required to do is disappointingly small. Once they leave school, however, for most young people there is a further sharp decline in the amount of reading they do, especially if it is not required as part of their job. Young people who were never very good at reading are at risk of becoming handicapped because of lack of practice. Later in life, some of them seek to obtain further help with reading, but it is an enormous effort—and the vast majority spend more time covering up the fact that they have reading difficulties than doing something about it. It is worth examining in some detail the learning competences that characterise each onward step in the development of reading.

DEVELOPMENTAL STAGES IN LEARNING TO READ

Up to age one

Children usually begin to: imitate sounds they hear in language; respond when spoken to; look at pictures; reach for books and turn the pages with help; respond to stories and pictures by vocalising and patting the pictures.

Ages one to three

Children usually begin to: identify and answer questions about objects in books, such as 'Where's the cat?' or 'What does the cat say?'; name familiar pictures; use pointing to identify named objects; pretend to read books; finish sentences in books they know well;

scribble on paper; know names of books and identify them by the picture on the cover; turn pages of board books; have a favourite book and request it be read often.

Age three

Children usually begin to: explore books independently; listen to longer books that are read aloud; retell a familiar story; recite the alphabet; begin to sing the alphabet song with prompting and cues; make continuous symbols that resemble writing; imitate the action of reading a book aloud.

Age four

Children usually begin to: recognise familiar signs and labels, especially on signs and containers; make up rhymes or silly phrases; recognise and write some of the letters of the alphabet; read and write their names; name beginning letters or sounds of words; match some letters to their sounds; use familiar letters to try writing words; understand that print is read from left to right, top to bottom; retell stories that have been read to them.

Age five

Children usually begin to: recognise and produce words that rhyme; match some spoken and written words; write some letters, numbers and words; recognise some familiar words; predict what will happen next in a story; identify initial, final and middle sounds in short words; decode simple words in isolation and in context; retell the main idea; identify details (who, what, when, where, why, how); arrange story events in sequence.

Ages six to seven

Children usually begin to: read familiar stories; sound out or decode unfamiliar words; use pictures and context to figure out unfamiliar words; use some common punctuation and capitalisation in writing; self-correct when they make a mistake while reading aloud; show comprehension of a story through drawings; write by organising details into a logical sequence with a beginning, middle and end.

Ages seven to eight

Children usually begin to: read longer books independently; read aloud with proper emphasis and expression; use context and pictures to help identify unfamiliar words; understand the concept of paragraphs and begin to apply it in writing; correctly use punctuation; correctly spell many words; write notes like telephone and email messages; enjoy games like word searches; use new words, phrases or figures of speech that they have heard; revise their own writing to create and illustrate stories.

Ages nine to thirteen

Children usually begin to: explore and understand different kinds of texts, like biographies, poetry and fiction; understand and explore expository, narrative and persuasive text; read to extract specific information, such as from a science book; identify parts of speech and devices like similes and metaphors; correctly identify major elements of stories, like time, place, plot, problem and resolution; read and write on a specific topic for fun and understand what style is needed; analyse texts for meaning.

The reader will immediately see that there are many elements here that could be focused upon using peer tutoring. We will turn now to examine the research evidence in a little more detail—but only from one paper (albeit one which looked at thousands of research studies and synthesised them).

THE RESEARCH BACKGROUND—BRIEFLY!

According to the report by the US National Reading Panel (NRP) (National Institute of Child Health and Human Development, 2000), the skills required for proficient reading are phonemic awareness, phonological skill, vocabulary, text comprehension and fluency. You will see how these mirror the various different ways that are individually promoted to teach reading—but the NRP is saying that all are necessary. Proficient reading does not necessarily require phonemic awareness as applied in Latin alphabets but an awareness of the individual parts of speech, which may also include the whole word (as in Chinese characters) or syllables (as in Japanese) as well as others, depending on the writing system being employed. Other important features distinguished in the report include a general understanding of the orthography of the language and practice.

Phonological awareness

This is the awareness of individual parts of speech as they apply to individual written characters —crucial for understanding reading (as defined by translating written characters into spoken language). Phonological awareness—which includes the manipulation of rhymes, syllables and onsets and rimes—is most prevalent in alphabetic systems.

Fluency

This is the ability to read orally with speed, accuracy and vocal expression. The ability to read fluently is one of several critical factors necessary for reading comprehension. If a reader is not fluent, it may be difficult to remember what has been read and to relate the ideas expressed in the text to his or her background knowledge. This accuracy and automaticity of reading serves as a bridge between decoding and comprehension.

Vocabulary

A critical aspect of reading comprehension is vocabulary development. When a reader encounters an unfamiliar word in print and decodes it to derive its spoken pronunciation, the reader understands the word if it is in the reader's spoken vocabulary. Otherwise, the reader must derive the meaning of the word using another strategy, such as making use of the context.

Orthography

This describes or defines the set of symbols used in a language, and the rules about how to write these symbols. Orthographic development proceeds in increasing complexity as a child learns to read. Some of the first things to be learned are the orthographic conventions, such as the direction of reading and that there are differing typefaces and capitalisation for each symbol. In general, this means that to read proficiently, the reader has to understand elements of the written language—including hyphenation, capitalisation, word breaks, emphasis and punctuation.

Practice

Repeated exposure to print improves many aspects of learning to read and most importantly the knowledge of individual words. It increases the speed at which high frequency words are recognised, which allows for increased fluency in reading. It also supports orthographic development, reading comprehension and vocabulary development. Peer tutoring usually substantially increases the amount of exposure to print and this is a key feature in its effectiveness.

Reading comprehension

The NRP describes comprehension as a complex cognitive process in which a reader intentionally and interactively engages with the text. It is essentially about understanding what the author intended the reader to learn when writing the text. Reading comprehension is heavily dependent on skilled word recognition and decoding, oral reading fluency, a well-developed vocabulary and active engagement with the text. Reading comprehension can be developed through: saying strategies before reading; exploring expectations of content; heightening motivation; establishing reading objectives; and activating previous knowledge and predicting content. When reading, consideration of the main ideas and self-monitoring can be helpful. After reading there can be summarisation and questioning of the understood text.

Of course, different methods do not all have the same effectiveness. For example, with respect to practice, research suggests that individual silent reading does not improve reading comprehension. What is key is the degree of challenge in the text and the amount and type of help received (Block, Parris, Reed, Whiteley & Cleveland, 2009). Thus, formal and explicit strategy instruction is required; this includes self-regulation and monitoring, questioning and capitalising on the help of others.

BRIEF THEORY: VARIATION ACROSS LANGUAGES

Because languages and scripts vary in multiple ways, it follows that models of reading need to consider different developmental pathways into proficiency. A typology of writing systems that has been popular for several decades is the threefold classification of scripts: logographic (written symbols represent an entire spoken word), syllabic (relating to or based on syllables) and alphabetic (a system where the alphabetic sounds are important). A problem with this narrow classification is that many of the world's scripts do not neatly fit into these categories. There are scripts that have mixed characteristics, such as the Indian akshara writing systems, which have both alphabetic and syllabic features.

Ziegler and Goswami (2005) drew together findings from across languages to explain reading development. They then proposed three contributing factors, not necessarily developing in this sequence. The first factor is the *availability and awareness* of different sound units prior to reading. The second factor is the degree of *consistency* seen in the associations between the sounds and the symbols of the language. The third factor is *granularity*, which refers to the level of mappings between the sounds and symbols in the language and whether they are smaller or larger sized units.

The authors consider reading development to depend upon the quality of mappings between orthographic units and the sounds of the language. They also argue that the nature of instruction is important for understanding reading development. If the correspondences between sounds and symbols are consistent and hence predictable, then learning the associations becomes easier. A faster rate of learning, it is argued, makes one script better than the other.

Within this view, scripts that contain predominantly one size of unit (e.g. Finnish with phoneme-level units) should be easier to learn than languages where mappings to symbol units are greater than one unit size. The contained orthographies of Latin-derived scripts comprise between 20 and 40 letters and the names and sounds of these letters are typically learned by the end of the first year in school (Seymour, 2005). English is often given as an example of a language with such multisized mappings in which minimal sound units (e.g. the phoneme [ai]) may be represented by single letters (e.g. *i*) but also by letter strings (e.g. *igh*). Such multiple mappings are seen as presenting a challenge to learners. The pace of learning depends on the size of the symbol set.

Leaving this brief theoretical interlude aside, and wondering how children ever manage such a difficult task as learning to read, we go on in the next chapters to more practical matters. The following chapter is about peer tutoring in general—some or maybe all of this will be new to readers. Then Chapter 3 is about peer tutoring specifically in reading—and getting to the heart of the reader's interest in this book.

2 PEER TUTORING

At school and in class we come across many situations where children work together, help each other and learn with and from one another. In the playground, one pupil helps to zip up the jacket of a toddler; students do homework together; one child shows a friend how to spell a word or how to do a sum; and so on. Generally, this help is provided informally and is spontaneous.

In the classroom, children can also collaborate in many more formal and deliberate ways. For example, they work together in small groups on an assignment; or a group assignment can be divided into several subtasks, where each group member is accountable for one of the tasks. In yet another form of collaboration, two students work together: one student provides the other with individual instruction or assistance in actively acquiring knowledge and skills. This type of collaboration, with a clear helping relationship between students, is called *peer tutoring* (Topping, 1996). Peer tutoring is one of the most frequently implemented and empirically studied formats of collaborative learning (Falchikov, 2001; Roscoe & Chi, 2008; Topping, 1996).

ORIGINS OF PEER TUTORING

Through peer tutoring children help other students at school with their learning, practising or rehearsing. This instructional technique of peers helping one another in learning contexts can be traced back to classical antiquity, when a tutor was essentially considered to function as a substitute teacher in a linear model of knowledge transmission from teacher to tutor to tutee (Topping, 1996). Since then, however, peer tutoring has been rediscovered in education on various occasions, with shifts in objectives and changes in focus on different actors.

In the late eighteenth and early nineteenth centuries, for instance, Andrew Bell and Joseph Lancaster developed a tutoring system in India and England, respectively, to address the discrepancy between the large numbers of students and a shortage of qualified teachers (D. Fuchs, L. S. Fuchs, Mathes & Simmons, 1997). They soon realised that this 'monitorial system' in which children taught other children was an important innovation in education. The Bell–Lancaster system almost immediately had a major international impact on the teaching practice of that time (Gerber & Kauffman, 1981). The advantages of peer tutoring for both involved students were immediately obvious, especially in the positive effects for the tutors. The idea was that 'to teach is to learn twice' and the fact that both students benefited from the collaboration still forms the foundation of present peer tutoring programmes (Vaessen, Walraven & van Wissen, 1998). Topping formulates a contemporary definition of peer tutoring as 'people from similar social groupings who are not professional teachers helping each other to learn, and learning themselves by teaching' (1996, p.322, emphasis added).

As a result of the growing number of teachers and their increasing professionalisation around the second half of the nineteenth century, the interest in peer tutoring decreased. However, from the late 1960s on, peer tutoring was rediscovered as an instructional strategy. Obviously, the historical and economic conditions had changed in the meantime, so that peer tutoring was no longer introduced because of the opportunity to teach large groups of students with a limited number of teachers. Rather, the renewed interest in that period was based upon the potential of peer tutoring to meet the needs of all children—including disadvantaged children—to increase the motivation and academic success of children with learning disabilities, and to reduce early school leaving and unqualified drop-out (Gerber & Kauffman, 1981; Vaessen et al., 1998).

Peer tutoring is now becoming increasingly more widespread and popular as an instructional strategy in education. Consequently, a diverse range of peer tutoring programmes have come to the fore. In this book we strongly suggest giving peer tutoring an even more central role in students' learning processes and experiences.

CONCEPTUALISATION AND TYPOLOGY OF PEER TUTORING

Peer tutoring programmes come in different shapes and sizes. This instructional strategy can be applied to all kinds of learning content and courses, as well as to various age groups. A teacher or school can use it for some weeks, or decide to implement it for a complete academic year, or for several consecutive years throughout the children's school career. Accordingly, Topping's (1996) definition of peer tutoring mentioned above covers a whole series of practices in which peers work one-on-one or in small groups to provide individualised instruction, practice, repetition and clarification of concepts (Duran & Monereo, 2005; Topping, 2005; Utley & Mortweet, 1997).

Topping (2005) more particularly distinguishes at least 13 organisational dimensions in the constellation of peer tutoring programmes which should be taken into account when designing and implementing such a programme: *curriculum content* (the knowledge and/ or skills aimed at in the programme); *contact constellation* (tutoring in a one-on-one setting or one tutor working with a group of tutees); *within or between institutions* (tutors and tutees from the same or different schools or educational levels); *year of study* (tutors and tutees from the same or different years of study or age); *ability* (same-ability or cross-ability tutoring); *role continuity* (the tutor/tutee role is permanent or exchanged throughout the programme); *time* (tutoring sessions in and/or outside regular class contact time); *place* (location of operation of the tutoring sessions); both *tutee* and *tutor characteristics* (all students or only a targeted subgroup of students involved); *objectives* (academic and/ or nonacademic aims of the programme); *voluntary or compulsory participation* of the students involved; and *reinforcement* (presence or absence of extrinsic reinforcement, such as certification, course credits, etc.).

Despite differences in format, intensity, curriculum content, objectives, etc., peer tutoring aims at 'the development of knowledge and skills through explicit active helping and supporting among status equals or matched companions, with the deliberate intent to help others with their learning goals' (Topping & Ehly, 2001, p.114, emphasis added). Furthermore, regardless of the variety of applications and manifestations in practice, peer tutoring is generally embedded carefully and structurally in the classroom organisation and in the curriculum and is characterised by specific role taking by the students: at any time one of the peers has the job of tutor, while the other is in role as tutee (Topping, 1996).

The *peer tutor* is more experienced or has more knowledge or skills and is expected to adopt a supportive role (Falchikov, 2001; McLuckie & Topping, 2004). In this respect, the tutor is supposed to create learning opportunities through questioning, clarifying, stimulating reflection and actively scaffolding another peer's learning (Chi, Siler, Jeong, Yamauchi & Hausmann, 2001; Duran & Monereo, 2005; Roscoe & Chi, 2008). The less experienced student receiving academic help and support from the tutor is called the *tutee* (Falchikov, 2001; Topping, 1996).

In addition to the role taking, the tutoring activities are generally characterised by clear procedures for interaction, in which participants receive generic and/or specific training and preparatory instruction (Topping, 2005). This is important since research shows that peer tutoring is less effective when no attention is paid to sound prior training of the tutors that is related to the content involved, or to necessary social and communication skills (e.g. Bentz & Fuchs, 1996; Ensergueix & Lafont, 2010; L.S. Fuchs, D. Fuchs, Bentz, Phillips & Hamlett, 1994; Topping, 2005). It is important to mention that tutor training is especially relevant for students with disabilities who take up the tutor role (Osguthorpe & Scruggs, 1986; 1990).

Different classifications of peer tutoring can be distinguished depending on the age of the students working together and on the continuity of the roles to which students are assigned. Children can be paired with peers from their own grade or class group in *same-age peer tutoring*, or with younger/older peers from other classes in *cross-age peer tutoring* (Duran & Monereo, 2005; Falchikov, 2001; Topping, 1996). Since differences in skills are stated to be more important than differences in age (Duran & Monereo, 2005; Graesser, Person & Magliano, 1995), reference is also made to *same-ability or cross-ability peer tutoring*, respectively.

In the format of same-age tutoring, the peer tutoring variant when children are grouped with classmates, tutors and tutees demonstrate comparable levels of expertise and development (Falchikov, 2001; Fantuzzo, King & Heller, 1992; Topping, 1996). In order to be successful, same-age peer tutors should be provided with additional information or resources to guarantee that they can really cognitively challenge their tutee's understanding (Falchikov, 2001; Topping, 2005). The specific form of same-age tutoring in which the students alternate on a regular basis between the tutor and tutee role is called *reciprocal same-age tutoring* (Cheng & Ku, 2009; Fantuzzo et al., 1992; Ginsburg-Block & Fantuzzo, 1997; Griffin & Griffin, 1998). This enables each involved student to experience the specific benefits of providing (in the tutor role) and receiving (in the tutee role) academic support, avoiding any social divisiveness according to perceived ability and status (Topping, 2005). Reciprocal peer tutoring is usually implemented in same-age settings (Falchikov, 2001; Topping, 2005).

However, most peer tutoring programmes engage older peer tutors to academically support younger tutees in cross-age and cross-ability tutoring (Falchikov, 2001). In the case of cross-age tutoring programmes, role reciprocity is not applicable, since it would be awkward and often impossible to alter the roles (Robinson, Schofield & Steers-Wentzell, 2005). Therefore, cross-age peer tutoring is generally *fixed peer tutoring*, where students operate as either tutor or tutee for the complete duration of the programme, without alternating their roles.

THEORETICAL FRAME OF REFERENCE

Current perspectives on learning increasingly emphasise the vital role of social interaction between learners for the development of knowledge and understanding. Since interaction and discussion are the core elements of peer tutoring, peer tutoring is primarily a social process (Chi et al., 2001; King, Staffieri & Adelgais, 1998; Roscoe, 2014; Topping, 1996) and matches this perspective. Both the individual cognitive perspective (Piaget, 1977) and the sociocultural view (Vygotsky, 1978) appear relevant, since each places social interactions at the centre of its theories of cognitive development.

From a *Piagetian perspective*, social interactions foster an intense examination of one's own competencies, leading to higher levels of reasoning and learning and to internalisation of academic goals (Rohrbeck, Ginsburg-Block, Fantuzzo & Miller, 2003). Piaget (1977) stressed the importance of interaction between peers because it helps children to 'decentre' and to become sensitive to perspectives other than their own. In this respect, researchers use the concept of 'sociocognitive conflict' to refer to how a child's understanding may be shifted by interacting with another child who has a rather different understanding of events. In order to comprehend each other and to solve these sociocognitive conflicts, peers need to discuss their originally contrasting understanding. The basic idea is that when two contrasting views are brought into contact, this is likely to stimulate cognitive restructuring, learning and improved understanding (Falchikov, 2001; Mercer, 1996).

By comparison, Vygotsky's *sociocultural theory* emphasises cooperation rather than conflict and suggests that cognitive development demands social interaction in more asymmetrical relationships with more capable others (e.g. peers, adults) (Falchikov, 2001; Hadwin, Wozney & Pontin, 2005; Mercer, 1996). Peer social interactions are filled with valuable exchanges of information and skills in which children adjust their cognitions through relating to others who may reflect differing language, behavioural styles and perspectives (Rohrbeck et al., 2003). More specifically, Vygotsky (1978) emphasised the transition from interpersonal to intrapersonal functioning and argued that social interaction may act as a stepping stone and even be a prerequisite for independent developmental achievement. What learners learn to do in interaction today, they will internalise and do independently tomorrow.

However, with a view to realising this, peers need to challenge each other in their 'zone of proximal development' (ZPD) (Chi et al., 2001; Hadwin et al., 2005; King et al., 1998). This notion of ZPD refers to the distance between what a learner can already do independently and a higher level, which can only be accomplished with the assistance of a more capable other (Mercer, 1996; Topping, 2005; Volet, Vauras & Salonen, 2009). Social interaction within a learners' ZPD promotes meaningful learning since it enables learners to bridge the gap between their actual and potential competences (Hadwin et al., 2005; King et al., 1998; Roscoe & Chi, 2008; Webb & Mastergeorge, 2003).

Notwithstanding the different theoretical approaches, these theories are not incompatible with one another. Each focuses on a different aspect of the interactive and collaborative process. Sociocultural theory, for example, can offer insight into the processes of students' collaboration to construct knowledge together. However, the concept of cognitive conflict must be borrowed from Piaget as a mechanism to explain individual cognitive change (Van Meter & Stevens, 2000).

Taking into account the importance of social interaction between learners acknowledged in current educational theories, the structure of the interaction in the one-on-one peer tutoring context appears especially promising and richer than the more traditional exchanges between teachers and students (i.e. teacher initiation of the dialogue, student response, teacher feedback). The next chapter, 'Peer Tutoring in Reading', will elaborate on this in more detail.

EMPIRICAL FRAME OF REFERENCE: PEER TUTORING EFFECTIVENESS

Apart from being one of the longest established and implemented formats of collaborative learning, peer tutoring is also frequently empirically studied (Falchikov, 2001; Roscoe & Chi, 2008; Topping, 1996). In addition to the wide-ranging possibilities for application of peer tutoring programmes, a broad range of positive effects are reported in the research literature as well. More particularly, peer tutoring has been proven successful in a variety of curriculum areas and for different age groups; and positive effects were found regarding both academic and social-motivational outcomes.

Numerous research results over the past four decades, both from individual studies as well as from systematic meta-analyses, convincingly point to improved student performance in various subject areas: spelling, reading, writing, mathematics, science, and so on (e.g. Bowman-Perrott et al., 2013; Cohen, J. A. Kulik & C. C. Kulik, 1982; Miller, Topping & Thurston, 2010; Oddo, Barnett, Hawkins & Musti-Rao, 2010; Rohrbeck et al., 2003; Van Keer, 2004; Van Keer & Vanderlinde, 2010). The research evidence regarding performance is too extensive to discuss here in detail; therefore, we will just have a closer look at two recent and methodologically sound meta-analyses focusing on student performance in particular. A meta-analysis merges different studies and analyses these jointly in order to synthesise and formulate overarching statements—in this case, regarding the effectiveness of peer tutoring.

The most recent meta-analysis of Leung (2014) included 72 articles on peer tutoring programmes including children and students from kindergarten to higher education. The findings demonstrate that peer tutoring has a positive impact on students' academic achievement. In particular, the studies in secondary schools displayed a larger effect size (i.e. a quantitative measure giving an indication of the magnitude of the impact of an intervention—peer tutoring in this case) than studies at other educational levels. Regarding the academic ability of the tutees, studies with high ability tutees displayed larger effect sizes than those with tutees of other academic ability levels, followed by low, average and mixed-ability levels. With respect to the academic ability of the tutor, studies with tutors of low ability displayed larger effect sizes than studies with tutors of other academic ability levels, followed by high, average and mixed-ability levels. Studies with 50% or fewer participants from minority groups revealed larger effects than studies with more than 50% minority participants. Same-gender dyads also displayed larger effect sizes.

The meta-analysis of Bowman-Perrott et al. (2013) examined the effects of 26 different research experiments for almost a thousand primary and secondary school students, indicating that moderate to large academic benefits can be attributed to peer tutoring regardless of the length of the intervention (i.e. the total number of hours students were involved in peer tutoring) and regardless of students' grade level or disability status. As to the latter, the findings reveal that among students with disabilities, those with emotional and behavioural disorders benefited most from peer tutoring.

Regarding these positive findings for students with disabilities, Bowman-Perrott et al. (2013) state that the fact that students with, or at risk of, disabilities demonstrate greater academic gains than their peers without disabilities or at-risk status may be reflective of the additional support they were provided with by means of peer tutoring—which they previously had not received. Also, other studies and meta-analyses disclose positive results of peer tutoring—both in the role as tutee and as tutor—for children with learning or behavioural difficulties and for children who are vulnerable because of their ethnic minority background (Bentz & Fuchs, 1996; Cook, Scruggs, Mastriopieri & Casto, 1985; Fuchs et al., 1997; Klingner & Vaughn, 1996; Mathes & Fuchs, 1994; Okilwa & Shelby, 2010; Scruggs & Mastropieri, 1998; Spencer & Balboni, 2003).

In addition to the aforementioned impact of peer tutoring on student performance, research also reveals other academic effects in terms of more deep-level learning (Ashwin, 2003; King et al., 1998; Loke & Chow, 2007; Topping, Campbell, Douglas & Smith, 2003), more frequent higher-order thinking (King et al., 1998; Roscoe & Chi, 2008; Topping & Bryce, 2004), as well as an increase in student involvement (Falchikov, 2001; Topping, 1996, 2005). Research also shows that peer tutoring interaction triggers students' metacognitive processes (i.e. students' thinking and reflection about their own thinking and learning) (King et al., 1998; Roscoe, 2014; Topping, 2001a, 2001b). More specifically, peer tutoring results in: increased knowledge about when and how to use particular learning and problem-solving strategies (Shamir, Zion & Spector-Levi, 2008); enhanced self-regulated learning (i.e. the conscious planning, monitoring, control and regulation of one's learning in order to optimise it) (King, 1998; Shamir & Tzuriel, 2004); and higher levels of self-control (Fantuzzo et al., 1992).

Notwithstanding the fact that nonacademic outcomes of peer tutoring have been studied somewhat less, social-motivational benefits are also reported in the research literature. More particularly, students' self-confidence, self-esteem, self-concept and sense of academic efficacy tend to be influenced positively, lowering students' distress (Cheng & Ku, 2009; Fantuzzo, Riggio, Connelly & Dimeff, 1989; Miller et al., 2010; Topping, 2001a, 2001b). Furthermore, students improve their social and communication skills, as well as their interrelationships, and tend to develop better attitudes towards school and the subject matter treated in the tutoring sessions (e.g. Ashwin, 2003; Cohen et al., 1982; Fantuzzo et al., 1992; Mathes & Fuchs, 1994; Robinson et al., 2005; Topping, 2001a, 2001b; Topping et al., 2003). Research also reveals students' appreciation for peer tutoring, both when providing and receiving academic help (Ginsburg-Block & Fantuzzo, 1997; Griffin & Griffin, 1998; Topping & Bryce, 2004).

In line with the underlying idea of peer tutoring—that peers help each other to learn and learn themselves by teaching (Topping, 1996)—research demonstrates the effectiveness of peer tutoring for both tutors and tutees. Studies even suggest that the positive effects of peer tutoring are greater for the tutor than for the tutee (Fitz-Gibbon, 1988; Greenwood, Carta & Hall, 1988). The latter confirms the assumption underlying the cross-age or cross-ability approach—that older and more able children can benefit from the peer tutoring experiences in their role as tutor for a younger or lower ability student. Consequently, it appears important to provide *all* students with the opportunity to be in the role of tutor as well as in the role of tutee (Robinson et al., 2005).

A possible explanation for this finding may lie in the fact that tutors are challenged to think through the learning content in more depth and from different perspectives, because they need to engage in questioning and explaining the learning content to someone else. This questioning and explaining something to others requires an in-depth reflection on the learning content (Roscoe & Chi, 2007, 2008). Consequently, having students tutor can develop their understanding and take tutoring knowledge and skills to a higher level (Ploetzner, Dillenbourg, Preier & Traum, 1999).

Therefore, based on the research literature regarding the effectiveness of peer tutoring, some important implications for implementation in daily practice can be formulated. First, as peer tutoring appears applicable and effective in many areas, it is worthwhile to consider implementing this instructional strategy in diverse subjects and fields and with different age groups, although in the remainder of this book we will deal specifically with peer tutoring in reading. Second, it is vital to implement peer tutoring for all children—at-risk or not, learning-disabled or not. Moreover, this recommendation also applies especially to the allocation of the tutor role, since the activities associated with this role in particular lead to positive outcomes. With good quality tutor training, engaging in the tutor role is valuable and fruitful for all children, not only for average or high achievers. Third, in formulating the objectives of your peer tutoring programme, think beyond just academic outcomes, since peer tutoring also has added social-motivational value.

FUNDAMENTALS AND PREREQUISITES UNDERLYING PEER TUTORING EFFECTIVENESS

As mentioned in the previous section, the research literature is optimistic and generally points out the benefits of peer tutoring. However, not all studies report unequivocal results and positive outcomes are not automatically guaranteed (e.g. Ashwin, 2003; Griffin & Griffin, 1998). Consequently, questions to ask are why, when and how is tutoring effective in promoting students' learning and skills? In studies on peer tutoring, emphasis is increasingly placed not only on the mapping of effectiveness in a variety of settings, diverse subject areas and age groups; but growing attention is nowadays also focused on the fundamentals and preconditions underlying peer tutoring effectiveness. In this respect, the ongoing processes and dynamics (i.e. what actually happens) during peer tutoring is increasingly the subject of research.

Research suggests a number of important instructional features explaining the success of peer tutoring for both tutors and tutees, especially its interactive nature and the one-on-one attention during peer tutoring activities—with both providing opportunities that can hardly be realised in traditional whole-class teaching. Peer tutoring involves extensive individualisation; more frequent and immediate feedback; reinforcement (i.e. praise and encouragement); error correction; increased involvement; academic engagement and time-on-task; and numerous opportunities to respond, to question and to be questioned (Bowman-Perrott et al., 2013; Ginsburg-Block & Fantuzzo, 1997; Greenwood & Delquadri, 1995; King-Sears & Bradley, 1995; Simmons, L. S. Fuchs, D. Fuchs, Mathes & Hodge, 1995; Spencer & Balboni, 2003; Topping, 2001a, 2001b; Utley & Mortweet, 1997).

Process studies of the interaction during peer tutoring activities show a diversity of pedagogical practices and strategies, such as: direct instruction; explaining; tutor modelling of thinking and problem-solving behaviour; fitting support to tutees' personal needs by means of scaffolding; asking questions or providing hints to elicit constructive and elaborative responses from tutees; and provision of immediate, positive and corrective feedback (Chi et al., 2001; Graesser & McNamara, 2010; Graesser, D'Mello, & Cade, 2011; VanLehn et al., 2007; VanLehn, 2011). As to students' questioning and explaining, thought-provoking questioning and knowledge-building explanations as opposed to factual questions and knowledge-reviewing explanations appear especially effective in stimulating meaningful learning (Graesser & Person, 1994; King, 1998; Roscoe & Chi, 2007).

Despite the potential of peer tutoring in terms of the opportunities for individualisation and high-quality interaction, just putting students together and hoping for the best does not necessarily guarantee productive learning for all learners (Topping, 2005). The success of peer tutoring is conditional upon the actual knowledge and skills of the tutor and upon the interaction dynamics in the pairs or groups (Topping, 1996, 2005; Webb, Ing, Kersting & Nemer, 2006). Because peer tutors do not often engage in highly interactive discussions and positive tutoring behaviours spontaneously in class, frequent explaining and questioning remains limited and superficial in nature (Chi et al., 2001; Graesser & Person, 1994; King, 1998; Person & Graesser, 1999). Consequently, providing peer tutors with assistance in tutoring skills and domain knowledge can help to realise more positive learning outcomes for both tutors and tutees. In this respect, research refers to the importance of embedding tutor training in the peer tutoring programme and/or supporting tutors with scripts or structured materials that shape the roles and activities related to the desired tutor behaviour (Topping, 2005).

Training peer tutors on intended tutoring behaviours before the onset of the tutoring activities has been shown to be successful and maximises the benefits (Falchikov, 2001; Fuchs et al., 1997; Roscoe & Chi, 2007; Topping, 1996). In the first instance, peer tutors and tutees should be informed about and encouraged to practise social and communication skills (Topping, 2005). Following on from this, peer tutors should be trained to focus on providing detailed explanations going beyond giving the correct answer, on thought-provoking questioning to stimulate tutees' deep reasoning (Graesser & Person, 1994; King et al., 1998; Roscoe & Chi, 2008; Webb et al., 2006) and on how to scaffold tutees' learning appropriately (Azevedo & Hadwin, 2005; Chi et al., 2001). In addition to the provision of introductory training, ongoing interim support for students is important to optimise their role taking (Falchikov, 2001; Schraw, Crippen & Hartley, 2006; Topping, 1996).

Another way of increasing the benefits of peer tutoring and facilitating learning is to provide students with scripts or structured materials to support the tutorial interaction, or to specify a sequence of interactive behaviour that can then be applied effectively to any materials (e.g. King et al., 1998; Fantuzzo et al., 1992; Miller et al., 2010). In this respect, the meta-analysis of Leung (2014) confirms that the adoption of structured tutoring indeed produces larger effect sizes than unstructured tutoring.

To conclude, the application possibilities of peer tutoring are wide and its potential and cost-effectiveness generally high. The latter more particularly refers to the fact that the benefits of peer tutoring exceed the costs associated with implementing this instructional strategy in daily practice. Implementing peer tutoring provides a great many opportunities to promote the learning of all students. Teachers in this respect take on a new role—of monitor, coach and facilitator—and should therefore create preconditions for high-quality peer interaction. Before presenting and elaborating on concrete examples of peer tutoring in reading in different international contexts, the following chapter will first focus in more detail on peer tutoring as a mechanism for the improvement of reading.

PEER TUTORING IN READING

WHY IS READING THE MOST POPULAR FOR PEER TUTORING?

It is fairly obvious why reading is the most popular subject for peer tutoring—reading is one of the most important skills or subjects children can learn in school. But there are more subtle reasons too. Reading is a skill that varies a little over the ages of the readers, but not as much as in other subjects. Maths, for instance, has a host of different areas which students have to learn more or less independently of each other. Reading, however, is a fairly homogeneous skill, and once you have the beginnings of it, you can improve by practising with feedback. Peer tutoring is often used to give students this kind of additional practice.

Peer tutoring through the developmental stages

Peer tutoring in reading varies with the developmental stage and age of the students. At the *preschool stage* little peer tutoring takes place, but many of the principles of peer tutoring are used by parents acting as tutors. Additionally, older siblings often act as helpers for younger children in the family. At the *primary stage* most peer tutoring focuses on comprehension of continuous prose, since teaching phonology is a somewhat complex task and also rather tedious, and is not generally considered very suitable for peer tutoring.

At the *secondary stage* there is even more emphasis on comprehension, focusing on longer and harder books and a wider range of reading materials beyond books. Peer tutoring pairs need to make rapid progress through substantial books, including some nonfiction books if they are indeed reading to learn. At secondary level, some schools have a scheme in which the oldest students in the school tutor the youngest—a kind of cross-age tutoring with a large gap in ability. The problem with this is that the tutors are unlikely to gain in reading skill—because of the large gap in ability. Deploying students two years older than the tutees is likely to be much more successful in yielding reading gains for both tutors and tutees, but secondary schools often find organising this much more difficult. Sometimes they revert to same-age tutoring within one year; this can be effective, but cross-age tutoring has a nurturing quality which makes it more likely to be effective. This issue will be elaborated on in more detail in the next chapters focusing on peer tutoring, both in general and in reading.

At the *adult level* peer tutoring is generally deployed with adults with reading difficulties (although it can certainly be used with any adult reading and any text which is a little too difficult for them). At this stage the adults should be encouraged to work with any text that is of importance to them—fiction, nonfiction, newspapers, written materials relating to their job, and so on. The peers can be drawn from an adult literacy class if the reader attends one, but many do not attend such classes. Outside of classes, it can be arranged for spouses, friends, workmates and other relevant peers to be trained to give such tutoring. This can often be arranged at all times of day at the convenience of the pair and, as such, fits more easily into the natural ecology of the partners. See Scoble, Topping and Wigglesworth (1988) for more details.

Using peer tutoring with any method of teaching reading

Importantly, peer tutoring can be organised so that it supplements whatever form of reading instruction is occurring in the classroom. This can be done by arranging for the tutoring to mirror the kind of reading instruction given by the teacher, being deliberately intended to give more practice in exactly what has already been taught in class. An example of this might be where a teacher believes that phonology is the best route to successful reading and not only teaches this in class, but also has tutorial pairs working purely on phonology.

An alternative model is to arrange to complement the reading instruction in the classroom, giving the pairs a wider experience of a different kind than the teacher can manage in direct class instruction. An example of this might be where a teacher teaches phonology directly in class, but also knows that phonology does not enable students to access more than half the words in the English language (for example), and that wider opportunities and experience of actually using phonological and other skills in reading continuous prose have to be offered.

A relevant factor here is the degree of control the teacher wishes to retain over the class. A teacher who is fearful of giving children too much freedom to learn might be more inclined to go with the first example, and have students practice things they have already learned in class in much the same way. However, a teacher with more confidence in their children might choose the second example, and be more inclined to enable the children to explore the borders of their own reading capability, albeit with the possibility that they will make some mistakes. In any event, making mistakes is more or less inevitable, since although tutees obtain much more individual attention during peer tutoring, of course the quality of that attention is much less than what a teacher would supply. So some sort of simple error correction procedure and arrangement for pairs to check on the correctness of what they are doing will form part of any peer tutoring procedure.

Reading with others requires reading aloud, which is functional (because it is the only way to share a text). It allows the development of accuracy, fluency and comprehension thanks to the sense of audience (knowing that someone is listening) and the feedback that the listener can offer. Pair interaction offers opportunities to develop meta-linguistic reflection (thinking and discussion about the language) and metacognition in general (in discussions with the partner about reading procedures), dialogue and thinking aloud, which is in line with studies that show that effective readers reflect and make decisions on their own reading process. In short, there is nothing to stop any form of teaching reading being supported by peer tutoring; it is simply a question of the teacher devising an appropriate tutoring technique and training the pairs in that technique.

PRACTICE AND EVIDENCE ON PEER TUTORING IN READING

As already pointed out in the previous chapter, peer tutoring promotes increased time-on-task, more opportunities to respond and regular and immediate feedback. This is especially true when peer tutoring occurs in a one-to-one relationship. In reading, there is evidence that the use of peer tutoring develops reading practice to three times that of traditional instruction (Mathes & Fuchs, 1994). Such features have encouraged the emergence of a rich range of educational practices, deploying new and effective methodologies. Some of these are based on research; others still anticipate research.

There are many initiatives that incorporate peer tutoring in order to improve reading. Many of them have not been collected in articles or books; others are linked to interesting local projects (like Samway, Whang & Pippit, 1995; Roller, 1998; Prescott-Griffin, 2005; Chipman & Roy, 2006); and still others have generated research about their practices. *Paired Reading*, *One Book for Two* and *Reading in Pairs* (to be explained in the next part of this book) are examples of the latter.

There are, of course, others and we mention some below.

- *Read On* (Topping & Hogan, 1999). This programme was designed to improve reading competence through peer tutoring, in order to stimulate motivation and pleasure in reading, as well as social skills and family involvement. The programme is based on *Paired Reading* and its abundant research, which will be explained in the next part of this book.
- *America Reads Challenge* (Wasik, 1997). This initiative promotes the participation of volunteers, usually students from secondary schools or universities, who act as reading tutors in schools. Volunteer tutors receive training in reading, vocabulary, writing and active listening. This initiative spawned a similar development in Scotland—*Scotland Reads* (Topping, 2006).
- *Reading Together* (Hattie, 2006). Developed in parallel in Israel (where it was known as *Yached*) and the United States, this programme aimed to improve fluency, comprehension and reading motivation with students aged 9 to 10 years acting as cross-age tutors of students aged 6 to 7.
- *Buddy Reading* (Shegar, 2009). This was a cross-age peer tutoring programme developed by Singaporean schools to increase the reading competence of children with reading difficulties. Pupils used the *Pause, Prompt and Praise* technique (Glynn, McNaughton, Robinson & Quinn, 1979). This technique will be explained in Chapter 8 in the next part, about *Reading in Pairs*, which also adopts it.

Meta-analyses

Although there are many studies that provide evidence about the effects of tutoring in the development of reading, for reasons of economy of space, we will only refer here to meta-analyses (a meta-analysis is a statistical summary of many studies).

The meta-analysis of Cohen et al. (1982) of 65 evaluations of school tutoring pro-grammes found an effect size of 0.29 for reading. (An effect size gives an indication from many studies of their average impact—the size of the intervention effect. Cohen (1992) suggests that effect sizes of 0.20 are small, those of 0.50 are moderate and those from 0.8 are large; this enables us to compare an experiment's effect size to known benchmarks.) Cook et al. (1985) reviewed 19 studies of peer tutoring in reading with students with dis-abilities. The effect size was 0.59 for tutors and 0.65 for tutees. Rohrbeck et al. (2003) examined 90 studies of peer-assisted learning in elementary schools with an effect size for reading of 0.26.

A meta-analysis conducted by Ritter, Barnett, Denny and Albin (2009) reviewed 21 studies of volunteer tutoring. Students who worked with volunteer tutors were likely to earn higher scores on assessments related to letters and words, oral fluency and writing, when compared to their peers who were not tutored. The effect sizes were relatively con-sistent, ranging from 0.26 to 0.45. Jun, Ramirez and Cumming (2010) analysed 12 studies with teenagers, obtaining an effect size of 0.26 on literacy. They concluded that this leads us to wonder not whether peer tutoring is effective, but why. More recently, Bowman-Perrott et al. (2013) carried out a meta-analytic review of 26 single-case research experi-ments in schools, with an effect size of 0.77 for reading, 0.74 for spelling and 0.92 for vocabulary. Findings thus suggest that peer tutoring is an effective intervention, regard-less of dosage, grade level or disability status.

Other key studies on reading

Besides these meta-analyses, recent research highlights the impact of peer tutoring in the development of particular aspects of reading competence: comprehension, speed, accu-racy, fluency and self-esteem (Miller et al., 2010; Oddo et al., 2010; Topping, Miller, Thurston, McGavock & Conlin, 2011). Other research emphasises the importance of teaching reading comprehension strategies explicitly (via activation of previous knowl-edge, predictions, hypothesis verification, identifying main ideas, monitoring and regulat-ing reading comprehension, and identifying text types and genres), as well as involving students in reading comprehension through interaction (Van Keer, 2004; Van Keer & Verhaeghe, 2005a).

PEER TUTORING WITH STRUGGLING READERS

There is thus evidence that peer tutoring has a positive effect on the development of reading. But why? And how can it benefit students with more difficulties? Ehri, Dreyer, Flugman and Gross (2007) showed that one-to-one tutoring, rather than small group instruction, was effective for teaching reading to struggling readers, because tutoring allowed instruction to be tailored to the individual needs of the learner, and because of the greater engagement in focused reading and practice with feedback. Tutors can engage learners with texts and learning processes for concentrated periods of time, focus the attention of young learners, model and scaffold reading and writing processes, provide immediate, individualised feedback in context and other personalised activities at key moments, and do all this repeatedly as may be needed (Juel, 1996).

These extensive opportunities to give and receive personalised pedagogical support show that peer tutoring is a privileged educational space for the development of students with difficulties in reading. It is an excellent methodology for inclusive education. The meta-analyses of Cook et al. (1985) and Bowman-Perrott et al. (2013) indeed confirm that peer tutoring is an effective method for students with disabilities, especially those with emotional and behavioural disorders.

Sideridis et al.'s (1997) study, which focused on students with difficulties in reading in primary education, also demonstrated the effects of peer tutoring in pupils with difficulties in spelling and social interactions. Results indicated gains for all students in spelling accuracy, an increase in the duration of positive social interactions and high satisfaction with the grades obtained. For students with disabilities, the gains in accuracy of spelling were double or triple the rates expected through traditional teaching.

Elbaum, Vaughn, Hughes and Moody (2000) meta-analysed the effects of different types of grouping (peer tutoring, small groups and multiple groups) for the learning of reading in students with disabilities. They contrasted this with the level of achievement reported in special schools. The results indicated greater effectiveness for reading comprehension in the alternative groupings, especially peer tutoring in comparison to traditional settings.

Ryan, Reid and Epstein (2004) reviewed 14 studies which examined the effectiveness of peer learning in different formats (cross-age tutoring, same-age tutoring, class-wide peer tutoring and cooperative learning) in children and youth with emotional and behavioural disturbances. The results showed benefits in all formats, with academic gains in reading and spelling. Peer tutoring is therefore seen to have positive effects for struggling readers.

USING CHILDREN WITH DIFFICULTIES AS PEER TUTORS

We have seen that the participation of students in vulnerable situations in peer tutoring activities benefits them. But can they act as tutors? Even as tutors of students without difficulties? This seems an important issue for children with difficulties in view of their feeling able to contribute on an equal footing. This concern was addressed by Cook et al. (1985): through a meta-analysis, they concluded that students with disabilities can be good tutors for peers with as well as without disabilities. Osguthorpe and Scruggs (1986, 1990) added that the only thing necessary is that they are suitably trained. However, as already discussed in the previous chapter, this is a precondition needed for peer tutoring success with any type of student.

Spencer and Balboni (2003) reviewed 51 peer tutoring studies involving students with intellectual disabilities. Results show that these students successfully played the tutor role and helped others in academic skills (reading, maths, grammar, lexicon and sign language) and skills for everyday life. The authors concluded that peer tutoring increased real-time work, promoted one-on-one instruction and gave opportunities for practice and feedback in a variety of areas and contexts.

There is also more research on vulnerable students (with autism or learning disabilities) or on students with disruptive behaviour (C. Maher, B. Maher & Thurston, 1998) acting as tutors. Shamir and Lazerovitz (2007) conclude that offering these students the opportunity to act as tutors can be a powerful instrument for effective participation in inclusive classrooms. Furthermore, in a review of studies of experiences of peer tutoring with vulnerable ethnic minority students, Robinson et al. (2005) concluded that the key lies in the creation of the pairs. The tutor role must not be reserved to the more competent students or those with high performance. The issue is to form pairs where the tutor knows a little more than their tutee, which gives rise to the opportunity for struggling students to tutor others who have more difficulties.

To summarise, students with difficulties can participate and learn in peer tutoring situations. However, it is necessary to make adjustments and offer support. Special support, when required, must remain in the classroom, but now with different objectives. There should be more emphasis on adjustment and on accompanying tutors before the peer tutoring activity, in order to promote mechanisms of mediation to the peer's needs; to help them regulate and monitor their own learning and that of their peer; and to prepare work in advance.

TEACHER SUPPORT TO TUTORS AND TUTEES WITH DIFFICULTIES IN READING

In situations of peer tutoring for the development of reading with students with difficulties or special needs, Duran and Valdebenito (2014) suggest that teachers:

■ Accompany and guide the student who works with a peer with difficulties by reviewing material in advance, anticipating possible problems, modelling teaching strategies and monitoring the tutoring session.

■ Fit the amount of time working on assignments and the tasks to the characteristics of the students. The teacher may guide the tutor in the addition or omission of some tasks; not all the pairs in the classroom necessarily need to perform the same tasks. Different settings are possible so that all students in the class share the goal of improving reading, but in different ways.

■ Adjust the materials; for example, some pairs will need a set text or work only with a summary or an alternative text, or with extra supports (definitions, pictures) that facilitate understanding.

Through peer tutoring, teachers can give opportunities to all students to participate and learn in the regular classroom. There is no reason for students with disabilities or special needs to be housed in different spaces or segregated classrooms. Cooperation between students engaged in the tutor and tutee roles, regardless of their characteristics, will create a network of mutual aid which will result in a true learning community. In this, each and every one of the students will be aware of the accomplishments generated and have social responsibility goals for themselves and their peers.

ADVANTAGES AND DISADVANTAGES OF PEER TUTORING

The first advantage of peer tutoring is, from our point of view, that it stimulates the development of cooperation among students. And we know how important it is that our students learn to cooperate, for this is an invaluable transferable skill in the knowledge society. From this general perspective we can highlight four elements:

1 Peer learning is a first-order strategy for inclusive education. The different formats of cooperative learning and peer tutoring in particular are a privileged methodology

for responding to diversity, because they take advantage of the differences among students. Students learn from one another precisely thanks to these differences.

2 Cooperation—or heterogeneous teamwork—is one of the three key competences for twenty-first century citizenship, as they are called by the OECD (Rychen & Salganik, 2001).

3 Cooperation, as students do in pairs in peer tutoring, also allows the development of complex social skills (active listening, mutual aid, agreement or praise) that can only be learned through working with others. These skills are fundamental for a democratic society.

4 Cooperation is, in addition, an engine of learning. All of us learn through the interaction with other people who know a little more than us and offer aid within our ZPD. Learning is not an individual achievement, but a product of social activity with other members who are more expert, and helps the learner to become more competent and autonomous. Cooperation allows learning with and from others (Wells, 1999).

The advantages of peer tutoring undoubtedly come from the educational potential that it has, compared with the limited individual assistance a single teacher can offer to each member of his or her class. It is impossible for the teacher to provide tailored or customised aid to each and every one of the students in the class. However, it is possible to arrange the classroom so that students in pairs can offer such personalised aid to each other. Good and Brophy (1997) argue that in these circumstances, peer mediation can prove to be more effective than adult mediation; while Greenwood, Carta and Kamps (1990) conclude that the mediation offered by one student in peer tutoring increases the quantity of pedagogical aid, the effective work time, the opportunities to respond and immediacy in the correction of errors.

The prototypical dialogue structure that characterises the interaction between a teacher and their student group is known as IRF, where the teacher initiates the dialogue (I), students respond (R) and the teacher offers feedback (F). The interactive structure in peer tutoring is richer and goes from a structure with three phases (IRF) to one with five phases (IRFCA) (Person & Graesser, 1999). In this structure, tutor and tutee follow the first three steps, but then tutor and tutee cooperatively improve the quality of the answer (C). Finally, the tutor evaluates the understanding of the answer (E). The fourth step of cooperation is the core of tutoring and explains its main advantages. The pedagogical strategies that tutors can put in place, because of their ability and the one-to-one scenario, arouse rich interactive mechanisms, some more tutorial (directed by the tutor) and other more collaborative (directed by both the tutor and tutee) (Duran & Monereo, 2005).

Taking into account the different interactive structure, Topping (2001a, 2001b) makes a comparison between peer-mediated learning and teacher-mediated learning. Peer learning enables a one-to-one relationship which explains the high levels of engagement (arousal, interactivity and engaged activity time). Peer learning also offers a communication that, although simpler, allows high levels of modelling, demonstration and personalised exemplification. The individualisation promotes great opportunities to question (and to be questioned), to receive and give immediate feedback and many other opportunities for reinforcement (praise and encouragement). Peer learning promotes autonomy, responsibility and opportunities for self-regulation and metacognition. And, finally, it can have a large effect on social and communicative skills, as well on self-esteem.

Research on peer tutoring shows clear benefits for the students—and not just for the tutee, who receives personalised support, but also for the tutor. We can summarise the advantages for the tutor in terms of:

■ Increased engagement, a sense of responsibility and self-esteem. The tutors feel that the tutee's learning depends on the help they give, which makes them emotionally involved. The quality of the relationship is their responsibility because of their role as tutor. It is an opportunity to be in the shoes of a teacher; they thus gain in responsibility and attitude towards school. The positive results of their tuition can help to improve the tutor's self-esteem.

■ Greater control of the content and better organisation of their own knowledge in order to be able to teach it. In line with research showing that teaching is a good way to learn (learning by teaching), preparing, explaining and monitoring the tutee's learning process is an excellent opportunity for more advanced or deeper learning by the tutor.

■ Awareness of gaps and inaccuracies and detection and correction of tutee errors. The instructional needs posed by the tutee allow the tutor to become aware of their own deficiencies and, at the same time, to learn how to detect the tutee's ones.

■ Improvement of psycho-social and interactive skills. The actions that emanate from the tutor role require learning and using social communication skills (such as paying attention or expressing with clarity) and helping skills (how to give time to think or ask questions).

On the other hand, the benefits to the tutee can be embodied in:

■ Academic improvements. Working with a tutor who offers personal pedagogical help implies an increase of study time, engaged work and greater motivation. These gains, as a result of the commitment to the peer, entail not only academic learning but changes in academic attitudes (like punctuality or attendance).

■ Psychological adjustment. Working with a peer can facilitate the reduction of anxiety, depression and stress, building an atmosphere of greater trust and confidence.

Beyond these advantages for students, Topping (1996) points out the further advantages for teachers and schools. The use of peer tutoring allows teachers to see in practice how students learn through their differences. In addition, it is an economic resource, which multiplies the sources of classroom teaching, makes learning more effective and allows teachers to offer individual or paired aid to those who need it. Finally, peer tutoring has political benefits in terms of democratically delegating the direction of the learning process, increasing students' autonomy and reducing dissatisfaction.

All the advantages and positive effects mentioned above have led to an expansion of peer tutoring educational practices and its academic recognition. For example, the International Academy of Education is a nonprofit organisation that promotes, in collaboration with UNESCO, the research, dissemination and implementation of pedagogical practices that improve education. They have placed tutoring among the ten most effective practices (Walberg & Paik, 2000) and published a monograph devoted exclusively to the subject (Topping, 2000).

However, it is clear that—as with all instructional strategies—peer tutoring entails disadvantages if it is not applied properly. Topping (2000) warns about these possible risks. As discussed above, peer tutors can provide a great number of individual aids that the teacher cannot, in the management of the conventional classroom. But the quality of these aids is, logically, poorer than teachers' aids and can lead to:

■ Failure to detect tutees' errors or misconceptions
■ Saying or showing incorrect information that reinforces these errors
■ Showing impatience and giving the answer to the tutee or doing the task for them, thereby greatly reducing their learning opportunities.

Fontana (1990) asserts that the main problem in misuse of peer tutoring happens by what he calls the easy option. Believing that we behold an instructional strategy of easy application, consisting of little more than putting students in pairs, could lead to the following drawbacks:

■ For tutors: overrating of oneself and of one's own skills; an excess of power and assertiveness; and emergence of a feeling of wasted time and lowered self-esteem, increasing if, in addition, tutees fail in their learning.
■ During the choice of pairs: a feeling of imposition and disinclination to be involved— and possibly student refusals.
■ A negative reaction from parents who retain the traditional or transmissible learning model and think that tutors are just being 'used'.
■ Perception of the school as an institution with poor resources. Surely with more teaching staff none of this would be necessary?

Fontana opts for a cautious and well-planned introduction of peer tutoring into a school. It is necessary to reflect on the implications for the school, the selection of subjects, students' characteristics, the kind of instructional activities available and the tutor profile. Finally, Greenwood et al. (1990) point out the main difficulty that peer tutoring faces: the conflict with the traditional concept of the teacher as the sole repository of knowledge and the linear transmission of knowledge. Both of these aspects will be revisited in the next part of the book.

DIFFICULTIES AND RESISTANCES TO USE BY TEACHERS, STUDENTS AND PARENTS

While we have pointed out the enormous potential of peer tutoring as a resource for more and better learning of our students, its incorporation into regular and systematic use in schools meets some difficulties. The success of peer tutoring practices depends on recognising, anticipating and finding ways to overcome these.

Many of these difficulties are common with other forms of peer learning, like cooperative learning, which, despite being one of the subjects most researched in educational psychology (D. Johnson & R. Johnson, 2009), experiences some resistance to being implemented widely. Different authors (Kagan, 2005; Rué, 1998; S. Sharan & Y. Sharan, 1994) coincide in pointing out the major resistances:

■ *Segmented school organisation or Taylorism.* The compartmentalised organisation (curriculum, staff, timetable and criteria for the assignment of groups and teachers), the linear programming, the textbook, etc., flow into an external and standardised control of students, based on individual and competitive learning.

■ *Students' perceptions about schoolwork*. In comparison with the individual work during the rest of the school day, some students can perceive cooperative activities as not properly academic or learning time. In addition, students the school has taught to compete may have difficulties in relationships within the teams.

■ *Degree of teacher's mastery of the new method*. Teachers must have a good grasp of the requirements: clear goals, positive interdependence, a well-defined group organisational structure and group assessment. All of these require training and practice.

■ *Professional attitudes*. It is necessary that teachers do not have a naive attitude (hoping only for advantages to prevail) and are patient for good results.

More recently, Y. Sharan (2010) recognised this paradox, defining cooperative learning as a valued pedagogy, but with a problematic practice, and suggested elements for overcoming it: educate teachers on the conceptual basis of peer tutoring, distinguish between the different methods and techniques, organise interactions between the members of the teams and develop a new role for teachers, exceeding the transmissive vision of teaching. The latter is surely the main challenge that peer tutoring faces: the traditional conception of teaching and learning based on the transmissive model, in which the teacher teaches (transferring information) and students learn. However, the current and modern ways of understanding learning and teaching are based on a sociocultural conception in which learning, even if it is individual, is built from social interactions with someone more skilful. This conceptualisation implies understanding that students can develop into the role of mediators (teachers) of their peers. But to make this happen, the teacher should share the last monopoly: the ability to teach. Teachers should trust their students and share the ability to teach with them. Teachers should stimulate situations in which students provide mutual teaching aid and, therefore, we must train and provide our students with resources so that they can act effectively as tutors of their peers.

The second big challenge, also derived from this new conception of teaching and learning, has to do with understanding that the complex activity of teaching others has a high potential for learning for oneself (Cortese, 2005). If we move away from the simple transmission of information and rephrase it, we can learn by teaching (Roscoe & Chi, 2007). If this principle, learning by teaching, is not understood by teachers, students and families, all of them will keep seeing the student tutor as someone who simply helps, but who misses opportunities to learn him- or herself. So peer tutoring could be seen as a bad instructional methodology, because it only appears to enhance tutee learning.

On the other hand, if we understand that we can learn by teaching (as the above mentioned research results show), peer tutoring becomes a powerful methodology capable of taking pedagogical advantage of the differences among students, and providing them with opportunities to learn by teaching (Duran, 2014).

PART

II

EVIDENCE-BASED GOOD PRACTICES

4 PAIRED READING
WHAT IS IT?

Because the term 'Paired Reading' has such a warm, comfortable feel to it, some people have loosely applied it to almost anything that two people do together with a book. Others have invented their own procedure, cheerfully (mis-)labelled it 'Paired Reading', then found it did not work too well, and looked around for somebody else to blame. Of course, the effectiveness researched only applies to 'proper' Paired Reading—that is, the specific and structured technique described below.

This dilution through problems of loose nomenclature and poor implementation can easily result in muddled attitudes to the technique. Indeed, in the USA, the need was felt to relabel 'proper' Paired Reading to try to avoid this kind of confusion. Teachers there felt the new name, 'Duolog Reading', was unusual enough to remain clearly identifiable in an educational market-place overwhelmed with a plethora of methods.

ELEMENTS OF *PAIRED READING* (PR)

The elements in the structure of the method are described below.

Selecting reading material

The tutee chooses reading material of high interest to them, from school, the community library or home. Newspapers and magazines are fine. However, if the tutee has a fanatical interest in one topic or type of book that is not shared by the tutor, some negotiation with the tutor will be needed, to avoid boredom for them.

Because PR is a kind of supported or assisted reading, tutees are encouraged to choose material above their own independent readability level. Tutees will not benefit if they select easy books within this level—but of course, the material must not be above the independent readability level of the tutor! To determine this, the pair can use the 'Five Finger Test' of readability:

- Open a page at random
- Spread five fingers
- Place fingertips on the page at random

- Tutor attempts to read the five words
- Repeat on another four pages
- If tutor has struggled on more than one word, the book is too hard.

The tutee can do something similar to check if the book is too easy for PR (in which case they could read the book independently at another time on their own if they so wish).

If the tutee becomes bored with the book they have chosen and wishes to change it, that is acceptable. If the book is boring, this is not the fault of the tutor, and the tutee should choose more carefully next time.

Contact time

Pairs commit themselves to an initial trial period of no less than 15 minutes per day at least three times per week, for an initial period of about eight weeks. It is best if there is consistently one main tutor to start with. Later, other peers, siblings, parents or grandparents—or even friends and neighbours—can help. However, they must all do PR in just the same way, or the child will get confused.

For peer tutoring, the three sessions per week should be in regular scheduled class time, with the possibility of doing more during break/recess if the pair wishes. This frequency of usage over the initial period enables the pair to become fluent in the method and is sufficient to begin to see some change in the tutee's reading.

Place and position

Finding a relatively quiet and comfortable place is desirable—not easy in a busy school or home! Pairs should keep away from televisions or computers and other distracting noise or activity.

It is important that both members of the pair are sitting comfortably together side-by-side and can see the book equally easily—tutors who get neck-ache get irritable! In the home, PR provides an all too rare opportunity for the parent (or other family member) and the child to get close to each other.

Discussion

Pairs are encouraged to talk about the book, to develop shared enthusiasm and to ensure the tutee really understands the content (without it seeming like a test). Of course, discussion makes noise, which should be taken into account (especially in a classroom setting).

Pairs should:

- Talk about the pictures
- Talk about interesting words or ideas or events
- Talk at some natural break—like at the end of a sentence, paragraph, page or section—or the tutee might lose track
- Review the main ideas or events at the end of chapters and at the end of the book.

In addition, the tutor should:

- Ask what the tutee thinks might happen next
- Listen to the tutee—tutors should not do all the talking.

Pointing

Tutors often ask, 'Should we point at the words?' The answer is not just 'yes' or 'no'; with a difficult book, or when the tutee is tired or not concentrating well, pointing might help—but tutors should only do it when necessary, not all the time. And if the tutee can do it rather than the tutor, that is preferable. Sometimes both can point together.

Correction

A very simple and ubiquitously applicable correction procedure is prescribed. When the tutee says a word wrong, the tutor just tells the tutee the correct way to say the word, has the tutee repeat it correctly, and the pair carry on. Saying 'No!' and giving phonic or any other prompts is forbidden. Tutors do not make the child struggle and struggle, or 'break it up' or 'sound it out'.

There will be some words that neither tutee nor tutor will know; tutors are not expected to know everything. Tutors must not bluff; if they do not understand, they must say so to the tutee. Then the tutee can ask a teacher or look it up.

Pause

However, tutors do not jump in and put the word right straight away. The rule is that tutors pause and give the tutee four seconds to see if they will put it right by themselves. Tutees will not learn to self-correct if not allowed the opportunity to practise this. Holding off for four seconds is not easy though, so tutors should be encouraged to count slowly to four in their heads before allowing themselves to interrupt.

The exception to this rule is with the rushed and impulsive reader. In this case, earlier intervention and a finger point from the tutor to guide racing eyes back to the error word is necessary.

Praise

Praise for good reading is essential; tutors should look pleased, as well as saying a variety of positive things. Praise is particularly required for:

- Good reading of hard words
- Getting all the words in a sentence right
- Putting wrong words right before the tutor does (self-correction).

PR does not proscribe undesirable behaviours (since that is usually ineffective) but instead, it promotes effective and desirable behaviours which are incompatible with the undesirable ones. A Dictionary of Praise can be found in the online Resources for PR.

Reading Together

So, how can the tutee manage this difficult book that they have chosen? Tutors support tutees through difficult text by 'Reading Together'—both members of the pair read all the words out loud together, with the tutor modulating their speed to match that of the tutee, while giving a good model of competent reading. The tutee must read every word and errors are corrected as above.

Signalling for reading alone

When an easier section of text is encountered, the tutee may wish to read a little without the support of Reading Together. At the start, tutor and tutee agree on a way for the tutee to signal for the tutor to stop Reading Together. This could be a knock, a sign, a nudge or a squeeze. The signal must be clear and easy to implement. When the tutee signals, the tutor stops reading out loud right away, while praising the tutee for being so confident.

Return to Reading Together

Sooner or later, while reading alone, the tutee will make an error which they cannot self-correct within four seconds. Then the tutor applies the usual correction procedure and joins back in Reading Together.

The PR cycle

The pair go on like this, switching from Reading Together to reading alone, to give the tutee just as much help as is needed at any moment. If the tutee has chosen a relatively hard book, more Reading Together will be needed and less reading alone. If the tutee has chosen a relatively easier book, less Reading Together will be needed and there will be more reading alone. Tutees should never 'grow out of' Reading Together—they should always be ready to use it as they move on to harder and harder books. If tutees seem to be doing a great deal of reading alone, it is probably a sign that the books they are choosing are too easy for PR.

Young able readers sometimes have difficulty accepting this switch from reading alone to Reading Together, as they are conditioned to assume that reading independently is the 'grown-up' way to read. In fact, of course, reading independently is only one way to read books, and then only books that are within one's current independent readability level. Also, no matter how good they are at the moment, everyone can always get better at reading—and this should be made explicit in training sessions.

Sticking to the 'rules'

Pairs should try to make sure they stick to these 'rules', at least for the initial period. If they do not, they are likely to get in a muddle. Each member of the pair should make sure they do not do each other's 'job'. It is the tutee who signals to silence the tutor from Reading Together—tutors cannot decide to go quiet when they feel like it. Also, when the tutee makes a mistake when reading alone, which they do not self-correct in four seconds, the tutor must correct it and go back to Reading Together. The tutee might ask for the tutor only to give them the word they were stuck on, and let them carry on reading alone—but that is not what the rules say!

ADVANTAGES AND DISADVANTAGES OF PR

PR has a number of advantages and remarkably few disadvantages. The advantages are given in Figure 4.1.

1   Children are encouraged to pursue their own interests in reading material. They have more enthusiasm from reading about their own favourite things, and so try harder. PR gives them as much support as they need to read whatever book they choose.

2   Children are more in control of what's going on—instead of having reading crammed into them, they make decisions themselves in the light of their own purposes (e.g. about choice of books, going on longer than ten minutes and going onto reading alone). They may never have had so much control before!

3   There is no failure—it is impossible not to get a word right within five seconds or so.

4   PR is very flexible—the tutee decides how much support is necessary according to the current level of interest, mood, degree of tiredness, amount of confidence, difficulty of the books, and so on.

5   The tutee gets lots of praise—it's much nicer to be told when you're doing well, instead of just being moaned at when you go wrong.

6   There's lots of emphasis on understanding—getting the meaning out of the words—and that's what reading is all about. It's no use being able to read the words out loud mechanically without following the meaning.

7   PR gives continuity—it eliminates stopping and starting to 'break up' hard words. Doing that often leaves children having forgotten the beginning of the sentence by the time they get to the end. With PR it is easier for children to make sensible guesses at new words, based on the meaning of the surrounding words.

8   When reading together, a child can learn (by example) to read with expression and the right pacing—for example, by copying how the tutor pauses at punctuation or gives emphasis to certain words.

9   Children are given a perfect example of how to pronounce difficult words, instead of being left to work it out themselves and then perhaps thinking their own half-right efforts are actually 100% correct.

10 When doing PR, children get a bit of private and peaceful attention from their own tutor, which they might not otherwise have had. There is some evidence that just giving children more attention can actually improve their reading.

11 PR increases the amount of sheer practice at reading that children get. Because children are supported through books, they get through them faster. The number of books read in a week goes up, the number of words children look at in a week goes up, and more words stick in the child's memory.

12 PR gives peers and parents a clear, straightforward and enjoyable way of helping their tutees—so no one gets confused, worried or bad tempered about reading.

13 ULTIMATELY, CHILDREN HAVE MORE INTEREST, CONFIDENCE AND UNDERSTANDING.

■ **Figure 4.1** Advantages of *Paired Reading*

PR FLOW CHART

A flow chart outlining the PR procedure is given in Figure 4.2. However, this is intended more for teachers and other leaders of PR projects than the children themselves.

RESOURCE MATERIALS

The resource materials on the website include specimen *How to Do It* leaflets for peer tutoring and for parents. You might wish to look at those now. You will also find some

PAIRED READING

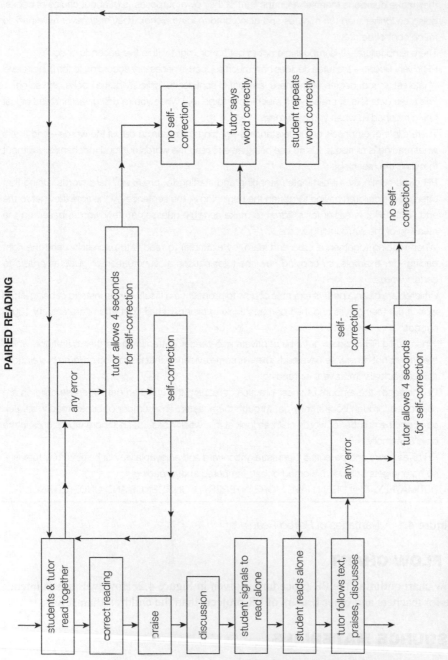

Figure 4.2 *Paired Reading* flow chart

overhead masters to use when presenting the method in staff development sessions or in training meetings.

THE NEED FOR PRACTICE

The best way to get to know PR is to actually do it. This applies to you as a professional as well as to those you might wish to tell about the method. Try to find a tame child or two who will let you practise on them. After this experience, this chapter and the method will make much more sense. Of course, you cannot make generalisations from a sample of one, so if you can practise on two or three children, this will be even better.

PR WITH NONREADERS

PR is designed to work with children who have already made some sort of a start with reading (typically a minimum sight vocabulary of 100 words or so). If you wish to use the method with tutees who are in the first stages of developing literacy, some adaptations are necessary.

A great deal more discussion to support understanding is necessary. You will need to control the readability of the books from which the pair choose to a much lower level, nearer to that of the tutee. If possible, you might create (or have tutors create) some personalised reading books for each tutee, including details and illustrations from the tutee's life experience. Encourage repeated reading of favourite books, with the tutor reading the book to the tutee on the first occasion, Reading Together on the second, then moving into full PR with increased tutee independence on each rereading.

OTHER LANGUAGES AND RESTRICTED LITERACY

With peer tutoring, in situations or families where the participants are bilingual, you might wish to have the leaflet for tutors translated into languages other than English. Examples of such translations have not been included in the Resources, because the list of possible languages would be very long and local dialects are so various.

You might feel as if such translation would be of little use in situations where many of the bilingual or ESL (English-as-a-second-language) population were not literate in their mother tongue. However, PR is very flexible and can be used in many ways. For instance, children might take home *How to Do It* leaflets in two languages and/or dual-language books and/or audio tape readings of single or dual-language texts. This can, for example, result in an aunt using PR to help the child and the parents learn to read the mother tongue, while the child uses the method to teach the parents to read English.

If you are working with families that are monolingual in English, in which it is difficult to find any member with a literacy capability any higher than that of the target child, you might wish to consider using texts of much more controlled readability, supported by audio tape readings. Of course, peer tutoring in school is an ideal way to manage this problem, but it does not quite have the warmth that you would hope for from a family setting. Another alternative is to use a volunteer parent to provide the tuition.

HOW DOES PR WORK?

Of course there is relatively little new about PR—some aspects of long-standing practice have merely been put together in a particularly successful package. However, it is this precise combination which has been proven. Remember, PR does not constitute the whole reading curriculum, but is designed to complement professional teaching without interfering with it.

In the United States, a number of approaches showing some of the features of PR have been developed over the years. These include *Reading-While-Listening*, the *Lap Method*, *Shadow Reading, Duet Reading, Assisted Reading, Prime-O-Tec, Talking Books* and the more fearsomely named *Neurological Impress Method*. Few of these were designed for use by nonteachers, however. Nevertheless, no single feature of PR is new. The effectiveness of the technique lies in the assembly and coherence of its elements—the total engineered package. The whole is more than the sum of its parts.

The PR method has a number of advantages. Some of these are common to other methods for parents or peers to help with reading, but many are specific to the PR method. When you are introducing the method to new users, the more curious of them may ask you questions about why the PR rules are the way they are. To help you answer such questions, and for your own information, you will want to be familiar with the content of the handout *The Advantages of Paired Reading*, shown in Figure 4.1 and on the website. Regard this as an optional handout for those who are deeply interested, otherwise you run the risk of drowning people with too much information.

The PR method obviously increases the amount of practice at reading, probably the most important factor in reading progress. Practice consolidates a skill, promotes fluency and minimises forgetting. Crucially, PR ensures that this practice is positive and successful. PR includes both modelling and scaffolding of correct reading, and thus provides a bridge between listening comprehension and independent reading comprehension. Good and weak readers typically differ much less in listening comprehension than they do in independent reading comprehension. Simultaneous reading and listening, as in Reading Together, is likely to free the struggling reader from a preoccupation with laborious decoding and enables other reading strategies to come into play. If the 'limited processing capacity' of the weaker reader is totally devoted to accurate word recognition or phonic analysis and synthesis, no processing capacity is left to deploy other strategies, such as using contextual clues.

However, while reading alone, the tutee is free to use whatever reading strategies they wish at any moment, strategically deploying a range of decoding or psycholinguistic strategies from word to word or sentence to sentence. They may use any strategies they have been specifically taught or strategies they have developed for themselves. Nevertheless, if they cannot select and successfully apply a strategy with the speed and fluency dictated by the four-second pause, the feedback and support of Reading Together switches in before the tutee becomes disconnected from the process of extracting meaning from the text. Thus, PR provides:

- ▪ Modelling
- ▪ Practice that is successful with extraction of meaning
- ▪ Scaffolding
- ▪ Feedback
- ▪ Praise and other social reinforcement
- ▪ Supported opportunities to experiment with the effectiveness of a wide range of reading strategies in a wide range of applications.

PR also:

- Enables the tutee to pursue their own interests and motivations
- Is highly adapted to the individual learner's needs of the moment
- Promotes learner-managed learning and self-efficacy
- Gives continuity—a 'flow experience'
- Eliminates the fear of failure in the tutee
- Reduces any anxiety and confusion in the tutor.

Many who have experienced PR liken it to how they learned to ride a bicycle. At first, learning to balance, steer and pedal simultaneously seems impossible, although each might be managed separately. However, with a parent or older sibling holding the frame and running alongside to share the balancing and steering burden, it quickly seems possible and before long is independently effortless.

Without a PR approach, there is some evidence that weak readers are likely to be interrupted more frequently and more immediately compared to fluent readers, and are more likely to be given phonic prompts for individual words. Such 'help' actually reduces the contextual and other psycholinguistic clues available to the reader and is likely to create learned helplessness.

PR is now acknowledged to have wide-ranging effects which are considered desirable by virtually all of the many different schools of thought on the teaching of reading. It is likely that different tutees benefit via different pathways or combinations of pathways. So attempts to find out which single route has the biggest effect for the largest number of children are probably only of academic interest.

A LINGUISTIC HEALTH WARNING

It should now be clear that '*Paired Reading*' is a specific name for a specific technique. It is not any old thing that two people feel like doing together with a book. Unfortunately, the name has become too widely misused. You will often meet people who say 'Oh, yes, we do that *Paired Reading*'. When you actually look at what they are doing, you often find that it is nothing like the specific method described above. So take care—just because you use the same name as someone else, it does not mean that the same ideas or practice are necessarily attached to the label. Take time to make sure that you are actually talking the same language.

BEYOND PR

Once pairs have learned the 'proper' PR technique, we would not of course want to deprive them of any freedom to experiment. After an initial period of consolidated practice, they may want to go back to reading independently for a while, or try some variant of PR, or try a completely different tutoring technique. The problem for a class teacher is that all pupils may want to do something slightly different, and this would become a big problem in terms of monitoring. So teachers should try to obtain a vote for the most popular method of continuing (or not) and then have all the class stick with that for a while. There is a 'Beyond PR' handout in the online Resources section.

5

PAIRED READING

DOES IT WORK?

There has been a great deal of research on PR, particularly in the UK, North America, Australia and New Zealand. It is one of the most intensively evaluated interventions in education; by the early 1990s, PR had been the subject of hundreds of studies. These were reviewed by Topping and Lindsay (1992a) and Topping (1995). The 1995 review is available in full on the eResources website, complete with all references. This chapter will briefly summarise the research on PR up until 1995, and discuss the research after 1995 in more detail.

PR is one of the most effective interventions in education. In a recent review of the effectiveness of 20 interventions in reading, PR is also ranked as one of the most effective, surpassed only by one or two methods which seemed to have produced spectacular results, but which had only been evaluated with very small numbers of children in research projects (Brooks, 2013). By contrast, PR has been demonstrated to be effective with thousands of children in hundreds of schools in many countries. Furthermore, implementing PR typically involves very modest additional costs in time and materials, with strong implications for relative cost-effectiveness.

OUTCOME RESEARCH TO 1995

Much of the evaluation research has been in terms of gains on norm-referenced tests of reading before and after the initial intensive period of involvement. The general picture in published studies is that Paired Readers progress at about 4.2 times 'normal' rates in reading accuracy in tests during the initial period of commitment. Thus, for example, PR for a three-month period was associated on average with gains in reading accuracy normally expected over a period of 12.6 3 × 4.2) months (although this is only an approximation, since it cannot be assumed that reading development is linear, and one month of gain in reading age would not mean the same from different reading age baselines). Gains in reading comprehension were even larger.

The research literature suggests that follow-up gains may vary considerably from school to school. Continued acceleration at above 'normal' rates is relatively rare and indeed, some follow-up gains cited are less than normal rates, while still remaining better than those of control or comparison groups. Follow-up periods have been various, ranging from 4 weeks to 12 months, but the length of follow-up does not appear to relate consistently to the favourability of follow-up findings. However, there is little suggestion here of 'wash out' of experimental gains; rather, there is evidence that acceleration can be sustained and even increased with the deployment of different types of tutor consecutively, and that changes in reading style can also endure in the long term.

These results are neither confined to isolated—and possibly atypical—research projects, nor to studies published in journals that might have a bias towards studies finding positive and statistically significant results. In the Kirklees school district in Yorkshire in the UK, the technique has been used by a majority of schools. This enabled study of outcomes in all projects in all schools. These unselected results are likely to give a much more realistic picture of likely outcomes in an average school under normal conditions.

In a sample of 2,372 children in 155 projects run by many different schools, average test gains of 3.3 times normal rates in reading accuracy and 4.4 times normal rates in reading comprehension were found. Although somewhat lower than the average from the research literature, this still represents a very substantial effect size. It was this effect size that the Brooks (2013) review compared with effect sizes from other interventions, not the higher effect sizes for PR indicated by the published literature (1.41 to 2.12).

The Kirklees results were supported by substantial baseline and control group data. In 23 baselined projects incorporating 374 Paired Readers who acted as their own controls, the difference between baseline (no-PR) and PR period gains was highly statistically significant. In 37 control or comparison group project studies incorporating 580 Paired Readers and 446 control children, the difference between PR and control group gains was highly statistically significant in both reading accuracy and comprehension—favouring the PR group, of course.

At short- and long-term follow-up, the gains of Paired Readers remained at above 'normal' rates on average, with no sign of wash out. At short-term follow-up (less than 17 weeks), 102 children in seven projects were still progressing at twice 'normal' rates of gain in reading accuracy and at 2.3 times in reading comprehension. At long-term follow-up (17 weeks to over one year), 170 children in 10 projects were still progressing at 1.2 times 'normal' rates of gain in reading accuracy and at 1.4 times in reading comprehension (see Topping, 1992a).

Children from all social classes were involved in the projects, with 60% of participants being of below-average socioeconomic status for the school district, which was itself disadvantaged. There was a tendency for participants of lower socioeconomic status to make larger gains in reading accuracy, even if not home visited. However, home visiting made an additional significant positive difference for participants in the lowest quartile of socioeconomic status. There are implications here for the cost-effectiveness of differential inclusion of home-visiting support in this kind of service delivery (see Topping & Lindsay, 1992b).

Children from families speaking English as a second or other language were recorded in 50 projects that yielded norm-referenced data, operating in 30 schools. Compared to Paired Readers for whom English was a first language, the ESL children made greater gains in accuracy (but not statistically significantly) and significantly smaller gains in comprehension, although the cultural relevance of the reading tests must be questioned (see Topping, 1992b).

More data were available for parent-tutored than peer-tutored projects, but no significant difference in outcomes between the two was found. The evidence suggested that tutors tended to gain more than tutees, although this difference did not reach statistical significance. There was less follow-up research on peer tutoring than parent tutoring. PR had also been used successfully with children with severe learning difficulties and other special needs and in further education and adult literacy.

Taking another approach to evaluation, the subjective views of tutors, tutees and teachers in the unselected projects were also gathered by structured questionnaire (Topping & Whiteley, 1990). In a sample of over 1,000 tutors, after PR, 70% considered their tutee was now reading more accurately, more fluently and with better comprehension. Greater confidence in reading was noted by 78% of tutors. Teachers reported generalised reading improvement in the classroom in a slightly smaller proportion of cases. Of a sample of 964 tutees, 95% felt that after PR they were better at reading and 92% liked reading more; 87% found it easy to learn to do; 83% liked doing it and 70% said they would go on doing it.

READING STYLE STUDIES TO 1995

Considering parent- and peer-tutored studies together, in eight studies, error rates have been found to reduce with PR and in no study have error rates increased. In seven studies, Paired Readers showed decreases in refusal rates and in two studies, an increase; an increase was shown in use of context in seven cases; in one case no difference was found; and in no case was there a decrease. In four studies, the rate or speed of reading showed an increase and in no case was there a decrease; and the self-correction rate showed an increase in four cases and in no case, a decrease. In three studies, the use of phonics showed an increase and in no case was there a decrease. Although many of the differences cited did not reach statistical significance—and only a few studies used either control or comparison groups who were nonparticipant or used another technique—strong consistent trends emerge from all these studies considered together.

The general pattern is of PR resulting in fewer refusals (greater confidence), greater fluency, greater use of the context and a greater likelihood of self-correction, as well as fewer errors (greater accuracy) and better phonic skills.

STUDIES OF COMPLIANCE TO TECHNIQUE TO 1995

In studies of compliance to the PR technique, many contradictory findings are evident for both parent-tutored and peer-tutored projects. High levels of compliance appear to be more likely in studies of smaller numbers of participants, especially when the training has been more detailed. In larger studies of parent-tutored PR at home, conformity to good technique has been found in 43 to 75% of participants, the higher figure being associated with home visits. Elliott and Hewison (1994) found that, even a year after training, working-class parents involved in PR showed greater comprehension-related discussion, more frequent rapid correction after brief pauses and less phonic correction, compared to an untrained working-class group. The working-class PR children could read as well as the middle-class children, while the untrained working-class children lagged behind.

The amount of time spent doing PR generally did not seem to correlate highly with measured outcomes, although measuring time-on-task in home-based projects is particularly difficult. Extra practice is clearly only one of the pathways through which PR has its effects. The vast majority of studies have evaluated on a crude input–output model, and the relation between technique compliance and outcome remains somewhat obscure.

STUDIES DIRECTLY COMPARING ALTERNATIVE METHODS TO 1995

Of 22 studies that directly compared PR to other techniques experimentally, in 18 cases, there was given statistical significance; and in seven of these, PR significantly out-performed other techniques. A number of other studies found PR superior, but the difference did not attain statistical significance in small samples. No study found PR significantly inferior. In the 15 studies yielding adequate norm-referenced data, the mean pre–post multiple of 'normal' rates of gain in reading accuracy for Paired Readers was 3.9, and that for other techniques, 2.7.

A META-ANALYTIC APPROACH TO COMPARING METHODS TO 1995

Alternatively, a meta-analytic approach to comparison could be pursued, comparing effect sizes in all PR studies with effect sizes in all studies using each specific alternative technique. Unfortunately, attempts to meta-analyse the literature on studies of 'hearing' or 'listening to children read' approaches quickly run into difficulties; of the major studies in the UK, one (Hewison & Tizard, 1980) found statistically significant effects, sustained at follow-up, while the other (Hannon, 1987) failed to find statistically significant effects.

A very large proportion of the other literature on 'hearing/listening' approaches fails to offer a precise description of what tutors were asked to do or actually did, and numerical outcome data are often conspicuous by their absence. However, crudely aggregating 14 published hearing/listening studies where reading test data are given (total n = 290) yields an average pre–post multiple of 'normal' progress of 2.53, compared to the PR literature average of 4.23. This latter finding on relative effectiveness is supported by reviews by Toomey (1991, 1993).

MORE RECENT STUDIES

Peer-tutored programmes

A programme of paired repeated reading was developed by Frost (1990) to improve reading comprehension in 14 third-grade students (aged 8 to 9). The 14-week reading programme involved a daily session of paired repeated reading incorporating critical thinking skills on alternate days. The Qualitative Reading Inventory was administered pre- and posttest. Results indicated that literal comprehension increased by 44%, main idea inference skills increased by 80%, and inference skills increased by 60%.

Leach (1993) investigated whether a PR programme had an effect on 10 third-graders. 'At-risk' readers identified 'more able' readers in the classroom. The 'at-risk' and 'more able' readers were paired as partners for a 16-week period, sharing and modelling read-ing strategies. The California Test of Basic Skills was used as a pre- and posttest, with a pre- and postattitude survey. There were substantial gains for tutees in achievement. Those tutees who had entered third grade reading below grade level were now reading at or above grade level. Results of the attitude survey showed attitudes of tutees were more positive as a result of the programme. Findings suggested that a PR programme is a manageable and effective classroom strategy that can be easily implemented to supplement varying teaching techniques.

A study with first-grade children (aged 6 to 7 years) was conducted by Muldowney (1995). For six weeks, a group of emergent readers was paired with more able readers, while another group of emergent readers in the same class was not paired. The two groups were tested before and after the project, using the Iowa Test of Basic Skills Level 6. The average gain of the Paired Readers was significantly higher than that of the non-Paired Readers.

Winter (1996) compared a peer-tutored PR class and a 'silent independent reading' (equivalent time-on-task at reading) class in each of three English-medium primary schools in Hong Kong. These children were very able readers. The PR tutees chose easy reading material, which they could read quickly with few errors. Unsurprisingly, error correction was very low. Nevertheless, the PR groups made much bigger reading test gains than the comparison silent reading class. Topping (1997) responded to issues raised by Winter and Monteiro (2013) tested the hypothesis that peer tutoring would benefit children's reading motivation. Participants were 80 fourth-graders and 80 second-graders from elementary school. The children who were to be tutored (second grade) were each paired with a helper from the fourth grade and a PR programme was developed. A questionnaire assessed reading motivation. There were statistically significant results favouring the children who participated: they showed significant increments in reading motivation, for both tutors and tutees.

A report on a cross-age peer tutoring PR strategy in primary schools in Antigua and Barbuda is provided by Warrington and George (2014). This began with the training of teachers in seven schools and was extended to all the schools on the islands in the following year. Qualitative research data from children and teachers showed that children were enthusiastic about the experience, with evidence that their wider interest in reading was stimulated. Although, for the pupils, the main benefit of PR was perceived to be an improvement in reading skills, for teachers it was the increase in children's confidence in reading.

Peer-tutored programmes for special groups

There are two studies which focused on PR with ESL populations and one that investigated PR with children with hearing loss.

Li and Nes (2001) investigated the effects of PR on reading fluency and reading accuracy in four ESL students with limited English proficiency. The students benefited from the PR intervention and demonstrated steady improvement in reading fluency and accuracy. This indicated that PR could serve as a useful instructional alternative to facilitate ESL students in learning to read in English.

A study by Pakulski and Kaderavek (2012) examined the effects of a reading intervention on narrative production, narrative comprehension and reading motivation interest in children with hearing loss. Seven school children between the ages of 9 and 11 were paired with younger 'reading buddies' (without hearing loss). The children with hearing loss read storybooks to an assigned reading buddy; these books included one narrative-style book and a matched storybook with manipulatives (i.e. felt board cutouts). Readings occurred for four days. Following the dyadic story readings, narrative production and comprehension were compared across the 'reading only' versus 'reading + manipulative' conditions. Data demonstrated that the 'reading + manipulative' condition resulted in significantly improved narrative quality and comprehension. Pre- and postassessment of the students' self-ranking of reading motivation and interest were also gathered and revealed a significant improvement in motivation and interest following the intervention. (This study used PR plus an additional treatment, as well as focusing on students with special needs.)

A longitudinal study conducted by Baker et al. (2012) examined the effects of a paired bilingual programme and an English-only reading programme on English reading outcomes for Spanish-speaking English learners (ELs) in first, second and third grades. Participants were 214 ELs enrolled in first grade (aged 6 to 7) in 12 high-poverty, low-achieving schools at the beginning of the study. Results indicated that ELs in the paired bilingual group made more growth on oral reading fluency in English than ELs in the English-only group across all grades. In general, ELs at risk for reading difficulties appeared to benefit more from the paired bilingual programme than ELs with moderate or low risk for reading difficulties.

Peer-tutored programmes with additional treatments

A second-grade class (aged 7 to 8) of 13 African-American students were involved in an intervention that consisted of PR and two interdependent group contingencies (Sharp & Skinner, 2004). All students began reading chapter-books and the number of chapter-book quizzes passed increased from an average of less than 0.70 per week during baseline to 7.5 per week during the intervention phase.

Huemer, Landerl, Aro and Lyytinen (2008) evaluated outcomes of two training programmes aimed at improving reading speed for 39 German-speaking poor readers in grades two and four. During a six-week training period, children in a PR group read books with an adult tutor. Children in a 'computer group' aimed to improve reading of word-initial consonant clusters by practice in associating an orthographic unit with a corresponding phonological unit. The results showed that both groups exhibited similar improvement. The PR group showed a more rapid gain in global word reading fluency than the computer group.

Peer-tutored programmes with multiple interventions

Here we mention studies which used multiple interventions where the effect of each intervention was not partialled out; thus, they do not provide strong evidence of the effectiveness of single interventions.

A programme for improving reading fluency was developed by Kartch, Marks and Reitz (1999). The targeted population was second- and third-grade students (aged 7 to 9 years). Fluency is not taught as a component of reading programmes. With most reading instruction focusing on comprehension and vocabulary, oral fluency does not develop enough for students to view themselves as readers. Four intervention strategies were selected: fluency modelling, PR, repeated reading and dramatisation. The intervention strategies contributed to substantial gains in students' reading fluency. The students' attitude towards reading improved and they became much more enthusiastic about reading aloud.

Bell and Caspari (2002) describe a programme for improving comprehension of non-fiction materials. Students of a third-grade class (aged 8 to 9 years) had difficulty reading and comprehending nonfiction material. The researchers noted that nonfiction is often perceived as being more difficult for elementary students to comprehend, and that strategies for reading and comprehending nonfiction materials are not consistently taught. Solution strategies included five interventions: more time spent with nonfiction; PR of fiction and nonfiction texts; graphic organisers to help students organise and synthesise information from the text; direct instruction of Collaborative Strategic Reading; and literature discussions using cooperative groups. A comparison of pretests with posttests showed a marked improvement in student scores.

A study of multiple interventions with parents was conducted by Ellis (1996), who utilised a pretest/posttest experimental design in a 12-week reading intervention with second- and third-grade students. Twenty parents randomly assigned to the experimental group participated in the weekly programme sessions, which emphasised simple techniques such as relaxed reading, PR and praise and encouragement. The 'Basic Reading Inventory' and 'The Self-concept as Reader' subscales of the 'Motivation to Read' scale were administered to the children before and after the intervention. Statistical analyses revealed significantly greater improvements in reading for the experimental group.

Parent-tutored programmes

Law and Kratochwill (1993) reported on a parent-tutored programme during the summer school vacation that incorporated very unusual recruitment, training and assessment procedures. No statistically significant improvement in reading accuracy or fluency from baseline to postintervention was evident (although the sample size was very small). However, the parents reported that the PR technique had a positive effect on their children's reading skills, particularly in increased confidence, interest, enjoyment and expressiveness. The majority of the children also rated the method highly.

Miller and Kratochwill (1996) recruited by repeatedly 'soliciting' parents of the students qualifying for 'Chapter One' reading services in two schools. Parents were trained individually, but several parents insisted on postponing training, while many others reported difficulty in getting started and continuing consistently. Many of the participating parents and students failed to cooperate fully. The subset of children in the PR condition, who actually completed the programme, did show significantly greater gains in accuracy and comprehension than their matched controls. These two studies illustrate the need to pay careful attention to organisational issues of implementation.

The first published study on PR from South America (Cupolillo, Silva, Socorro & Topping, 1997) sought to evaluate the PR procedure with children who were repeating first grade in an area of northern Brazil where 55% of the population was illiterate. Tutors included parents, relatives and peers, but all tutoring took place in homes. The project was evaluated in terms of tutee changes in reading fluency, comprehension, confidence and reading habits. Gains were evident for those who had participated consistently, especially in confidence and reading habits. This novel use of PR with young, emergently literate, children in a very different cultural context (and continent) was ground-breaking, though some adaptation of the method was involved.

DeAngelo (1997) implemented an action research project for improving the reading skills of at-risk middle school students (fifth- and seventh-grade). A review of solution strategies resulted in the selection of PR using parental involvement with daily oral reading and an incentive programme. Postintervention data indicated an increase in students' reading comprehension scores and in increase in the participants' speed and accuracy reading scores.

A PR programme in a disadvantaged community in Cape Town, South Africa, was reported by Overett and Donald (1998). Parents and other family members served as tutors for students in English-medium classes. Experimental and control children were on average a year behind their chronological age in reading accuracy, and two years in reading comprehension. More than half the children reported there were no books in the home and of the remainder, very few had more than two books in the home. Experimental and control classes received equivalent loans of books, and class teachers encouraged both groups to join the library. Compared to the control group, the PR group made statistically significant improvements in reading accuracy and comprehension, as well as reading attitude. Relationships between tutees and tutors improved, and other children in the families seemed to benefit also. Interactions between family, school and the local library were enhanced.

Murad and Topping (2000) reported a further study from Brazil, with children attending first grade (aged 6 to 7 years) for the first time, but in a relatively advantaged private school setting. All tutors were parents and a control group of children, who had no PR training, took equivalent books home to read with their parents. Although similar at pretest, PR children were significantly superior to their controls at posttest, especially in relation to the deeper complexities of the logical sequence and meaning of the text. Autonomous reading fluency was also higher for the PR group. There were indications that the affective and self-efficacy components of PR were particularly important.

The effectiveness of a PR intervention using curriculum-based measurement (CBM) probes to document student reading progress was undertaken by Fiala and Sheridan (2003). Parents and children used the PR method in their homes for 10 minutes, four times a week. Results showed that the children's reading accuracy and rates increased from baseline to follow-up on CBM measures and pre- and posttesting.

In a pretest/posttest control group design, parents in an experimental group received reading materials and were trained on techniques to stimulate their child during PR at home, while a control group only received materials (Cadieux & Boudreault, 2005). Reading and general academic abilities were pre- and posttested, along with phonological awareness and self-concept. The results showed statistically significant gains in general academic abilities and phonological awareness in favour of the experimental group.

A PR programme was implemented for 195 Hong Kong preschoolers (mean age 4.7 years) and their parents (with a wide range of family income) (Lam, Chow-Yeung, Wong, Lau & Tse, 2013). The preschoolers were randomly assigned to experimental or waitlist control groups. The parents in the experimental group received 12 sessions of school-based training on PR in seven weeks. They were required to do PR with their children for at least four times in each of these seven weeks. At the end of the programme, the preschoolers in the experimental group had better performance in word recognition and reading fluency than their counterparts in the control group. They were also reported as more competent and motivated in reading by their parents. More importantly, the programme had many favourable effects on parents. Parents in the experimental group had higher self-efficacy in helping their children to be better readers and learners. They also reported that they had better relationships with their children. Their changes in relationships and self-efficacy were found to mediate the programme impact on some of the child outcomes. However, family income did not moderate the effectiveness of the programme. Families with high and low income alike both benefited from the programme.

Shah-Wundenberg, Wyse and Chaplain (2013) investigated parental support for children's reading of English in an inner-city school in the developing country context of an Indian city, Ahmedabad. Children had oral proficiency in the regional language but were beginning to acquire conventional forms of literacy in English. A quasi-experimental trial with a sample of 241 children was conducted to assess the relative effectiveness of two approaches to parents supporting reading: PR and Hearing Reading. Both were found to be equally effective in enhancing children's budding English reading skills, reading accuracy and comprehension, relative to controls. Parents engaged in a variety of mediation behaviours to enhance their children's English reading development. Parents felt that participating in their children's reading was both enriching and empowering.

THE 'READ ON' PROJECT IN SCOTLAND

The Read On website at the University of Dundee in Scotland has further information about this project: www.dundee.ac.uk/eswce/research/resources/readon.

In the PR phase of the pilot Paired Reading and Thinking project in Scotland, the equivalent of 32 full classes in 13 schools were involved in cross-age peer tutoring. Older primary school students (around 10 or 11 years of age) tutored younger students of around 7 or 8 years of age. Pairs met three times per week for 20 minutes per session, over a 10-week period.

For tutees in sixteen full classes, nine classes showed average gains well above normal, which reached statistical significance; six classes showed gains above normal, which did not reach statistical significance; and one class showed only normal gains. For tutors in sixteen full classes, seven classes showed gains well above normal, which reached statistical significance; eight classes showed gains above normal, which did not reach statistical significance; and one class showed only normal gains. The majority of children in this project were in disadvantaged schools and their scores before the project started were well below average in many cases—in other words, what was a 'normal' rate of gain for most children was not normal for them. The aggregated gains for all tutors were highly statistically significant. The same was true for the tutees.

A minority of schools were able to provide nonparticipant control or comparison groups of the same age for either tutors or tutees. One school managed to provide both, and the results are displayed in Figure 5.1. Both PR tutors and tutees out-performed their respective controls.

An analysis was conducted of the relationship between pretest reading ability and amount of reading test gain. Overall, the tutees and tutors who were the least able gained most. Low ability tutors produced tutee gains at least equivalent to those produced by high ability tutors—and low ability tutors themselves gained more than high ability tutors.

The relationship between reading gains and gender was also analysed. Overall, female tutees did better than male tutees, but male tutors did better than female tutors in terms of their own test gains. So, perhaps boys learn better by being tutors than by being tutored. Teachers had been encouraged to match children by ability differential, disregarding gender; but nevertheless, cross-gender matching proved to be less usual. However, cross-gender matching actually yielded better tutee gains than same-gender matching, and was good for tutors as well. Male–male pairs appeared very good for the tutor, but not for the

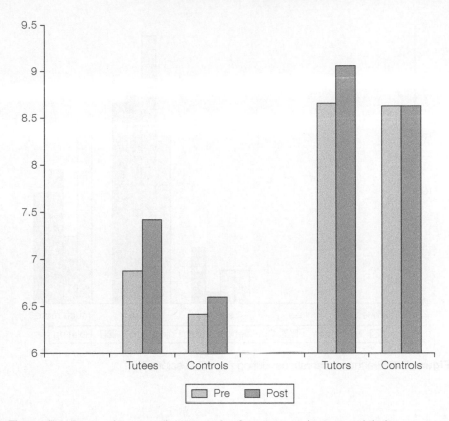

■ **Figure 5.1** Pre- and postreading age gains for tutees and tutors and their controls

tutee (contrary to previous findings of high gains for both partners in this constellation; see Topping & Whiteley, 1993). Female–female pairs did least well on aggregate.

Social gains were also widely reported. Each participating teacher was asked to record their summary observations of child behaviour. They were asked to comment only on children in their class whose reading they knew before PR started, and only indicate change if they had observed that it was significant and had definitely occurred since PR started. The response rate was 33 out of a possible 34 (97%—one teacher had left the school). The summary results are displayed in Figure 5.2 for behaviour in the classroom during PR, and in Figure 5.3 for behaviour in other activities in the classroom and outside the classroom within school.

It is clear that for behaviour in the classroom during PR, very few teachers had not observed a positive shift in the majority of their children. Regarding generalisation of positive effects to other subject areas and outside the classroom, the effects were not as strong (as would be expected), but were still very positive. The improvement in motivation during the PR sessions was particularly striking. Especially worthy of note was the improvement in ability to relate to each other—and that the children's social competence improved both during PR and beyond it.

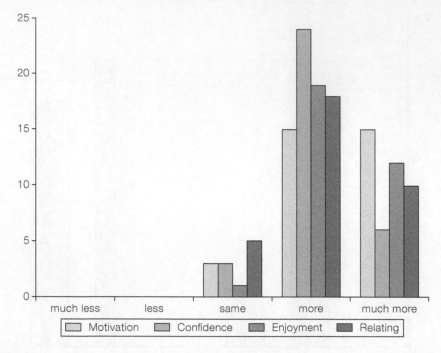

▪ **Figure 5.2** Teacher observations: during the PR sessions

THE FIFE PEER LEARNING PROJECT

Many of the previous studies were small-scale studies in situations where the teachers volunteered or self-selected to participate. So how representative could they be of all schools, including those where the teachers were preoccupied with other issues? The Fife Peer Learning Project considered peer tutoring in reading, encompassing 80 schools (with children aged 9 and 11 years), and followed children for two years (involving teachers from two consecutive classes), randomly allocating intervention types and assessing quality of implementation. All the primary schools in a school district (143 of them) were asked if they wanted to take part in an intervention project, which was a randomised-controlled trial—in other words, if they agreed, they would have an intervention randomly assigned to them, which was not of their choosing.

Amazingly, 129 schools agreed to participate. The intervention was intended to explore the effects of tutoring in reading or maths, or reading and maths, same-age or cross-age tutoring (tutees and tutors from the same class or from different classes separated by two years), and light (once per week) or intensive (three times per week) intervention. Thus, 12 types of intervention were randomly assigned to schools (see Table 5.1). This occurred for 15 weeks (January–April) and was repeated in the second year for the same pupils, many of whom had a new class and new teacher. It is easy to operate an intervention project with a few selected teachers and schools, who are likely to make almost anything a success. The randomisation of interventions here was testing

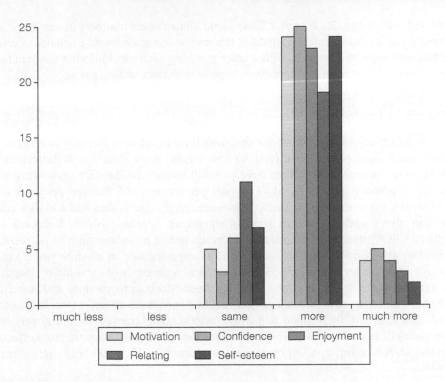

■ **Figure 5.3** Teacher observations: outside the PR sessions

the effects on teachers and schools whose motivation was not heightened by being able to choose the nature of the intervention. This was therefore a much more rigorous test of the intervention.

The intervention types particular to this study (same-age or cross-age, light or intensive, reading, mathematics or reading and mathematics tutoring) have been discussed somewhat in the previous literature.

Cross-age versus same-age tutoring

Regarding cross-age or same-age tutoring, Cohen et al. (1982) found cross-age tutoring showed greater effects than same-age tutoring; Britz, Dixon and McLaughlin (1989) found cross-age tutoring more common than same-age tutoring, although the latter was more common with older pupils. Reviewing peer tutoring for pupils with emotional and

■ **Table 5.1** Skill areas, types of peer tutoring and intensity of intervention

	Same-age	Cross-age
Reading	Intensive/Light	Intensive/Light
Mathematics	Intensive/Light	Intensive/Light
Reading and mathematics	Intensive/Light	Intensive/Light

behavioural disorders, Ryan et al. (2004) found almost equal numbers of same-age and cross-age studies. Spencer (2006) updated this review and again found a balance of cross-age and same-age studies, some of the latter involving reciprocal tutoring (switching of roles of tutor and tutee on a regular basis, usually with same-ability pairs).

Intensity of tutoring

There is still much to learn about the optimum level of tutoring intensity. Cohen et al. (1982) found short programmes (zero to four weeks) most effective. Rohrbeck et al. (2003) found 'dosage' varied from three to 1,080 hours—the duration of tutoring with elementary school pupils averaged 47 minutes per session, 3.65 sessions per week over 15.35 weeks, but with great variance. Below-median dosage studies had a higher effect size than above median, but this was not significant. Ginsburg-Block, Rohrbeck and Fantuzzo (2006) found that duration of intervention had no relationship to outcome in elementary schools; Ryan et al. (2004) found average duration of sessions was 25 minutes and total number of sessions 33, but there was no analysis of outcome by length of intervention; while Robinson et al. (2005) reviewed tutoring programmes and noted that both short- and long-term tutoring projects could demonstrate effectiveness; and Leung, Marsh and Craven (2005) found that while more sessions (more than three) per week were more effective than fewer, shorter sessions (under 30 minutes) were more effective than longer. Regarding duration of programme, more than 12 weeks was slightly better than less.

Summary

Thus, cross-age tutoring is more common than or equally common to same-age tutoring and appears to be more effective. Regarding intensity, the evidence is mixed and equivocal. Nothing could be found in the literature on the relative effectiveness of tutoring one or two subjects, but this was considered of interest in case additive effects were found from tutoring two subjects.

Research questions

1   Does peer tutoring using PR lead to gains in tested reading achievement compared with pupils not participating when the treatment type is randomly allocated?
2   Does the effectiveness of this tutoring vary according to intensity of tutoring, same-age or cross-age tutoring or whether single or dual subjects were tutored?
3   Does effectiveness vary according to gender, socioeconomic status or reading ability?
4   Are there factors in the process of PR which particularly contribute to developing gains in reading?

Method

The study took place in a school district in Scotland of mixed socioeconomic status with 143 primary schools. On average, each experimental school had 235 pupils and 241 controls. Schools were various in numbers of pupils (38 to 542), as the school district encompassed both urban and rural environments. Incidence of free school meals (widely used as an indicator of socioeconomic status of schools in the United Kingdom) for intervention schools was 17.5% and for controls 16.1% (compared with the average of 17.5% for the whole school district and 16.9% for Scotland). There were very few ethnic minority pupils.

Thus, the classes involved were predetermined (except where there was more than one class of the specified age within the school, when one was selected randomly). In small schools where a single class contained pupils of two or more year groups, pupils not in the targeted ages were included in the intervention or not, as the teacher decided, but further data on them were not gathered. The teachers involved represented the full range of age and experience. In some cases, teachers participated somewhat reluctantly, having been 'volunteered' by their head teacher.

Library provision differed between schools—some smaller schools struggled to offer a wide range of nonfiction and fiction books; while some, but not all, bigger schools had a large, organised, levelled library at either classroom or school level or both, from which the tutoring pairs could choose.

Training

At the first continuing professional development (CPD) session, at least two class teachers came from each school, joined in many cases by the head teacher or other staff—yielding 450 teachers in one room. The session involved a context-setting talk from a senior manager of the school district, an outline of the rationale and importance of randomised-controlled trials, and a talk about the tutoring technique and how to organise it. Then, by dividing the teachers into 12 smaller (but still large) groups representing the different types of intervention, we created opportunities for networking between schools about to use the same type of tutoring. A resource pack was made available to all schools. It referred briefly to operational definitions and the research background, but mainly consisted of practical materials for teachers to give to pupils and organisational advice for the teacher her/himself.

After the first intervention period, the teachers had a further half-day of CPD, involving presentations from teacher colleagues who had implemented successfully and a further opportunity to feed back and discuss. The CPD was repeated in the second year for new teachers, adding the use of a demonstration video and brief presentations from two selected first-year schools. Research assistants were available to support schools in achieving high fidelity of implementation, but they did so only on request, by visiting schools individually or by holding discussion sessions for a group of schools. In these visits and sessions they were thus working with the teacher's definition of the problem, not the problem as they had observed it themselves. Further details can be found at www. cem.org/fife-peer-learning-project.

Organising the tutoring

In cross-age tutoring between two classes of different ages, pupils in each class were ranked by reading ability (according to teacher judgement or test results and sometimes both), and the most able tutor in one class matched with the most able tutee in the other class, and so on. In same-age tutoring, one class was ranked by reading ability, divided into tutors in the top half and tutees in the bottom half, and the most able tutor matched with the most able tutee, and so on. The purpose of matching in this way was to sustain a similar modest reading ability differential in each pair, which previous studies had found was the most effective way of maximising gains for both tutee and tutor. Thus in same-age classes, the weakest tutee was helped by an average tutor; while in cross-age classes, the weakest tutee was helped by the weakest older tutor. In the latter case, the weaker pairs might need extra coaching from the teacher. Small matching adjustments were made on grounds of social compatibility. Further information on organisation is available on the eResources website.

Parents were informed of the project and given the opportunity to withdraw their child if they wished. A few parents had further questions, which were addressed, but no one withdrew their child. Teachers then instructed tutors and tutees together in the PR tutoring technique. Teachers were asked to tell pupils about the structure of the technique and give a demonstration of how to do it. Tutoring pairs then immediately tried out the technique with a book of appropriate difficulty, while teachers circulated to monitor and coach. Teachers continued this monitoring and support during the subsequent reading periods (a teacher checklist for observation was made available—see the eResources website for a copy of this). Pairs kept a brief written record of their reading. Absence of pupils for any session left teachers needing to rematch unpartnered individuals.

Measures

Long-term achievement data gathering occurred six months before the first academic year of participation and six months after the second academic year of participation. Short-term achievement data gathering occurred pretest in November/December and posttest in May, in both years. Posttests were administered in schools in roughly the same order as the pretests, so that similar timescales were involved. Implementation quality data gathering occurred in February for both years, and all observations were contained within a three-week period. A few schools dropped out or changed type of intervention and had to be eliminated from the study, but this did not greatly affect the results.

The long-term evaluation used one group reading comprehension test (Performance Indicators in Primary Schools) with all pupils (n = 8,847), comparing them to all pupils of that age in Scotland. The short-term evaluations examined pupil performance in 15 randomly selected schools (n = 494) with five control schools (n = 211), using the NFER Group Reading Test in the first year and the Suffolk Reading Test in the second (alternative tests were used to explore whether even more significant results could be obtained—but they were more or less the same). These were sentence reading tests requiring the pupil to select the correct word from four alternatives to complete the sentence—arguably comprehension and word focused. Different schools were randomly selected for the second year.

In addition, researchers undertook direct observation of implementation using a structured observation schedule (or protocol) in 50% of randomly selected schools in both years, since it is worthless to obtain an effect in outcome evaluation without evidence that the intervention was actually implemented. This was also to explore questions such as: Did the teachers absorb all or some of the brief pretraining? Did they implement it in their training of pupils? Did they monitor and follow-up appropriately over time?

Finally, self-esteem was investigated—the extent to which involvement as tutor or tutee made pupils feel better about themselves. Eight schools were randomly selected equally from same-age and cross-age schools (238 pupils). Controls were chosen at random from schools in a neighbouring school district (162 pupils). Rosenberg's Self-Esteem Scale was used for 11-year-olds and a shortened version of the Harter Self-Perception Profile for Children for 9-year-olds, requesting responses on a Likert scale to questions about pupil perceptions of their personal worth.

Results

First, did the tutoring work? On the long-term evaluation, yes—but only with cross-age tutoring (the effect size was 0.22—small but important). Effect sizes were very similar for the older (tutors) and younger (tutees) pupils involved in cross-age tutoring. Thus, cross-age reading tutoring had a modest effect for both tutors and tutees when measured over a very long time period. The modest nature of this effect is unsurprising in a large randomised trial, where effect sizes are often smaller than in smaller studies with selected schools. On the short-term evaluations using different reading tests, however, same-age and cross-age tutoring did equally well. In the first year of reading, the intervention group did significantly better than the control group (effect size = 0.31), with the reading and maths tutoring intervention type significantly superior. Low socioeconomic status and lower reading ability pupils gained significantly more, as did girls. In the second year of reading, the intervention group again did better than the control group (effect size = 0.34). Low socioeconomic status pupils, lower reading ability pupils and the reading and maths intervention type were significantly better. Girls were almost significantly better (Tymms, Merrell, Andor, Topping & Thurston, 2011).

However, observation of implementation quality was important. Table 5.2 shows that some behaviours were much more frequent than others. The first four behaviours concern technical aspects of correction, and these behaviours were frequently observed. Tutor mis-correction was very low, which is good. Of the next four behaviours, three concern

■ **Table 5.2** Aggregated frequencies of behaviours observed per school

Behaviour	Minimum	Maximum	Total Mean per school	Standard deviation
Mistakes made	4	32	15.62	7.97
Tutor repeats words correctly	2	34	13.68	8.18
Pause 4/5 seconds exactly, then correct	2	32	13.56	7.91
Tutor goes quiet straight away	0	23	8.74	9.16
Show interest in book	5	10	8.35	1.27
Talk about the content	0	56	7.18	12.85
Tutee repeats words correctly	0	32	7.15	9.42
Talk in reading together and alone	0	15	4.29	3.48
Reading together exactly	0	11	1.91	3.42
Tutor praises	0	20	1.82	4.86
Tutee signals for reading alone	0	7	1.29	2.31
Tutor praise during reading alone	0	7	0.53	1.70
Tutor mis-corrects	0	2	0.24	0.56
Tutor praises for going alone	0	1	0.18	0.39

interest in the book and talking—these behaviours were somewhat frequent. However, Reading Together Exactly, Tutor Praising and Tutee Signalling were all relatively rarely seen—all major aspects of the PR technique. We may conclude that implementation was somewhat variable (Topping, Thurston, McGavock & Conlin, 2012).

Interestingly, significantly more mistakes were observed in same-age than cross-age pairings. Mistakes then drove the use of the error correction process and same-age tutors corrected more errors. Class gain in reading test score was plotted against the mean number of mistakes per minute. This indicated that there was an optimum rate for mistakes—about one mistake every two minutes. Same-age pairs also tended to stop and talk about the book more during reading. When talking was plotted against reading test score gain, there were greater gains when the pair stopped reading to talk about the book between every five to seven minutes (not more frequently, although less made little difference).

Significant gains in self-esteem were seen in both same-age and cross-age pairings, for tutees and tutors, but not for controls. These gains reflected improved beliefs about reading competence. In addition, the scores of cross-age tutors showed further gains in wider self-worth, indicating that working with younger tutees provided extra benefits (Miller et al., 2010).

Practical implications for teachers

Cross-age tutoring is worth trying out in primary schools, because it appears to have long-term effects. It may be more difficult to organise than same-age tutoring, and requires cooperation between two teachers, but larger effects can be expected from volunteer teachers than from those in this study. Importantly, there are effects for both tutor and tutee (a double gain), a point that should be made to the parents of those involved. However, shorter-term results suggest that same-age tutoring also has benefits. Consequently, teachers might wish to try out tutoring on a same-age basis before progressing to cross-age tutoring. Children of low socioeconomic status, lower reading ability pupils and girls gained significantly more.

Some of this is encouraging news, as teachers are particularly concerned about the first two groups, and clearly these kinds of pupils should be included in projects. The finding of better progress for girls does not address concerns about lower reading performance in boys, and further thought is needed about this issue. Of course, boys who do PR may still do better than girls who do not do PR. This study did not analyse by the gender of the pair, but it might have been that same-age tutors were more likely to be girls and tutees more likely to be boys, which may be a factor.

The role of self-esteem here is important. Pupils may gain partially from the effect of extra positive reading practice—but equally so from the enhancement to their self-esteem from working with a partner, particularly (though by no means exclusively) as a tutor. This emphasises the value of involving lower reading ability pupils as tutors in a cross-age project. Teachers may wish to work on enhancing the value of peer tutoring in the eyes of the pupils so that this effect might be increased.

Teachers will seek to raise the quality or fidelity of intervention. Some aspects of technique were good, but teachers need to pay particular attention to monitoring and coaching with respect to Reading Together Exactly, Tutor Praising and Tutee Signalling. More mistakes are evident in same-age tutoring, so here teachers need to be particularly vigilant. Perhaps same-age pairs are more likely to choose books that are too hard for them.

The optimum rate of mistakes (one per two minutes) is something for teachers to watch out for when monitoring PR sessions. Likewise, talking about the book every five to seven minutes can be a focus of monitoring and coaching.

Pupils involved in two types of intervention (reading and maths tutoring) were likely to make larger gains than those only involved in one, so there seems to be some additive effect (although reading and maths tutoring methods were quite different). However, teachers will struggle to find time to implement two types of tutoring simultaneously, so this finding is of uncertain practical worth. Of course, this does not prevent them from implementing the two forms consecutively.

Training for teachers is necessary and more than the half-day of training in this study would be desirable, preferably spread over time. This training should incorporate practice and feedback. Subsequent direct independent observation of the teachers implementing would be good, but would add to costs considerably. A less costly alternative is for a pair of teachers within a school to observe each other. Interestingly, intensity (high or low) made no significant difference, confirming the equivocal previous findings in the literature. However, teachers need to be careful in assuming that low intensity will always suffice. In the early stages of implementation, pupils need to be practising PR more frequently than once per week if they are to become fluent with the method.

Beyond this, the study has demonstrated the value of thinking big, evidencing effectiveness on a large scale even when the nature of the intervention was forced upon schools. It seems that the PR technique is robust and resilient to surviving deployment in schools where it might not at first be welcomed. School districts might wish to ponder whether such district-wide initiatives have advantages, although of course schools might already be implementing practices for which they have good evidence.

SUMMARY AND CONCLUSION

The primary point to make is that PR 'works'—in terms of raising scores on all kinds of reading tests, improving attitudes to reading and enhancing self-esteem—and there is evidence that these gains are sustained. PR has demonstrated a high degree of durability, replicability and generalisability, in a wide variety of contexts in many different countries. Despite methodological weakness in some of the reported studies, the better quality studies have shown no less encouraging results than the rest. In any event, the sheer volume of multiple-site replication is impressive.

Secondly, PR generally works better than regular class teaching alone, and better than supplementary silent reading, or peer- or home-based 'listening' to reading approaches. Thirdly, exactly why and how PR works remains somewhat mysterious. Positive changes in reading style have been noted in Paired Readers, but it is not clear whether these are causes, effects or mediating mechanisms. However, the conception of PR as a unitary intervention might be over-simplistic. The PR experience might offer participants multiple pathways to improvements in multiple aspects of the reading process. Thus, different components of the technique might be most potent for different readers, reducing the probability of finding a few process factors which are omnipotent for all.

Recommendations for further research include more multiple-site field trials of improved quality. This is increasingly occurring in an international context. Meanwhile, it may be concluded that PR has certainly been better evaluated than many educational innovations.

It has been argued that community interventions should be:

- Simple
- Inexpensive
- Effective
- Compatible with the existing values and need structures of the population
- Flexible
- Decentralised
- Sustainable.

The research on PR is generally most encouraging and suggests that, in a context of well-organised service delivery, the technique is capable of meeting all of these requirements.

6 ONE BOOK FOR TWO
WHAT IS IT?

BASIS AND AIMS

Reading comprehension

Becoming a skilful reader is an important goal in primary education, providing valuable tools for future learning throughout one's school career (Guthrie & Cox, 2001). Being a competent reader is, however, not only required for success at school, but also crucial for adequate participation in our information society (Netten, Droop & Verhoeven, 2011; OECD, 2004). Learning to read is therefore one of the most central learning processes children are involved in at primary school.

Becoming a proficient reader is, however, not easy or undemanding for all students. That is because reading is a complex process and successful reading requires many skills in which children can fail. Although phonics, word reading and reading fluency are important building blocks of literacy, reading comprehension is unquestionably the ultimate goal of reading instruction. Without comprehension, reading for pleasure and knowledge is out of the question (Vaughn & Linan-Thompson, 2004).

Unfortunately, however, it is especially this ultimate goal of reading comprehension that many children appear to persistently struggle with. In this respect, reading instruction seems not always able to handle students' comprehension difficulties adequately; and across the world, schools are confronted with a continuous challenge to improve students' reading skills—with the key question being how to teach children effectively to extract meaning from text. Taking this challenge into account, *One Book for Two* explicitly focuses on fostering reading comprehension in primary school children, by combining explicit instruction in reading comprehension strategies and peer interaction in cross-age peer tutoring pairs.

Need for explicit instruction in reading comprehension strategies

Comprehension is the active process of extracting and constructing meaning from text (Snow & Sweet, 2003; Van den Broek & Kremer, 2000). Proficient readers do more than process words, phrases and sentences—they flexibly make use of different comprehension-monitoring and fostering activities (Dole, Nokes & Drits, 2009; Van Keer, 2004). They set goals for reading, recognise the author's purpose, monitor comprehension while reading, reflect on the ongoing reading process and evaluate their understanding. Furthermore, they draw on a variety of appropriate strategies to handle comprehension difficulties (Van Keer &Vanderlinde, 2013). In this respect, skilful readers are characterised by their application of both metacognitive and cognitive strategies (Dole et al., 2009; Guthrie, 2003; Pressley & Harris, 2006).

Cognitive strategies are mental and behavioural activities used to increase the likelihood of comprehending; for example, rereading, activating and retrieving prior knowledge, adjusting reading speed, making inferences and linking key ideas (Van den Broek & Kremer, 2000; Vellutino, 2003). Metacognitive strategies are self-monitoring and self-regulating activities, focusing on the process and product of reading, such as: readers' self-awareness of whether or not they comprehend what they read; their ability to judge the demands of a task; and their knowledge of when and how to employ cognitive strategies, taking into account text difficulty, situational constraints and one's own cognitive abilities (Dole et al., 2009; Pressley & Harris, 2006; Van den Broek & Kremer, 2000).

Regrettably, not all students spontaneously develop knowledge about these strategies and the competence to select and apply appropriate strategies just through practice—that is, immersion in varied reading materials and by doing lots of reading (Hartman, 2001). Quite the reverse: research indicates that teachers and schools need to provide all students with systematic support throughout their school career in the active comprehension processes and strategies used by skilled readers, aiming at improved comprehension and literacy. More specifically, studies refer to explicit instruction in comprehension strategies as an effective and feasible approach in this respect (e.g. Alvermann, Fitzgerald & Simpson, 2006; Van Keer, 2004; Van Keer & Verhaeghe, 2005a).

Explicit instruction refers to teachers' intentional activities to instruct children in which strategies are relevant, as well as in how and when to use them in diverse situations. In daily educational practice, however, asking content-related questions after reading a text is still dominant over explicit instruction and modelling of the comprehension strategies needed to answer the questions posed (Aarnoutse & Schellings, 2003). Moreover, as strategy instruction moved into classroom practice, it is believed that much of the fidelity of strategy implementation has been lost; and it is not certain that these efforts have resulted in effective strategy instruction in classrooms today (Dole et al., 2009). For this reason, explicit instruction in reading comprehension strategies is included as one of the cornerstones of *One Book for Two*.

Need for peer interaction about texts

In addition to the value of explicit reading strategies instruction, research points to the importance of opportunities for students to participate in peer interaction about texts as a way to optimise reading strategy use (RSU) and comprehension (Almasi & Garas-York, 2009; Alvermann et al., 2006). The conventional interaction patterns during reading comprehension lessons (i.e. teacher question, student response, teacher evaluation) appear not to be effective enough. This type of interaction implies that there is a single, correct interpretation of the text—so students accordingly await the teacher's evaluation and become passive learners (Almasi & Garas-York, 2009; Cazden, 1986). In contrast, students need to take an active role when reading, monitoring and regulating the reading process and comprehension (Almasi & Garas-York, 2009). Active reading can be fostered by engaging students in peer interaction about texts. In this respect, children not only talk about what they are reading, but also about what they *do* when reading; consequently, students learn about, implement and evaluate the use of reading strategies.

Taking the above into account, one might expect teachers to implement peer interaction and discussion on a regular basis during reading comprehension activities. In reality, however, this does not seem to be the case. Peer interaction regarding texts is anything but common practice in most classes (Alvermann, 2000). In *One Book for Two*, we recognise the gains from peer interaction for fostering reading comprehension and include cross-age peer tutoring as one of the cornerstones.

DESCRIPTION AND PROGRAMME CHARACTERISTICS

With *One Book for Two*, we aimed at rethinking and redesigning reading comprehension instruction in primary schools. Intending to close the gap between the above mentioned reading research evidence and the educational reality of reading comprehension instruction, we developed an innovative approach, encompassing two complementary cornerstones: explicit instruction in reading strategies on the one hand; and creating opportunities to engage in meaningful peer interaction and collaboration regarding reading books and texts, on the other. We more specifically opted for cross-age peer tutoring to put peer interaction about texts into practice, with fifth- and sixth-graders (aged 10 to 12) taking the role of tutor of second- and third-grade tutees (aged 7 to 9) respectively.

The programme began in Flanders (the Dutch-speaking part of Belgium), and student material and a teacher manual were developed in close cooperation with pilot schools and teachers (Van Keer, 2002; Van Keer & Vanderlinde, 2008). The teacher manual includes a general description of the background, aims and organisation of the *One Book for Two* project; lesson scenarios describe the objectives, necessary materials, preferable instructional techniques and the successive phases of each lesson; and these are used together with supplementary student materials, such as strategy assignment cards and reading texts. The different elements of the project are explained and illustrated in more detail below.

Explicit instruction in reading comprehension strategies

Compared to traditional reading comprehension instruction, the major changes in *One Book for Two* regarding explicit reading strategies instruction relate to the *content* of teaching and learning on the one hand, and to the *instructional strategies* used on the other.

In terms of the content, based on a review of related research and descriptions of the reading behaviour of proficient readers—and in line with the Flemish standards and curricula for primary schools—we selected the following reading strategies as relevant and feasible for primary school children targeted in the One Book for Two project:

1 Activating prior background knowledge and linking it to the text
2 Predictive reading and verifying the predictions made
3 Distinguishing main ideas or essentials from side ideas or details
4 Monitoring and regulating the understanding of words and expressions

5   Monitoring and regulating comprehension in general
6   Classifying text genres and adjusting reading behaviour to them
7   Making a graphic summary or scheme of the text (solely included for third- and sixth-graders).

By activating prior knowledge, students bring to mind what they already know about the theme or topic of the text before reading. This activity is generally considered to be advantageous for text comprehension. In *One Book for Two*, we particularly teach students to deduce the subject of the text on the basis of the title and pictures, to think about what they already know about that topic, and to write down a number of key words in a word web. In this respect, they frame the content of the text in a larger whole of knowledge and information.

Text comprehension requires the reader not only to activate prior knowledge, but also to use it in integrating ideas and meaning across sentences, paragraphs and various parts of a text. This is called inferencing and both the second and third selected reading strategies in *One Book for Two* depend on skills, such as applying and integrating prior knowledge and understanding relations between parts of a text. With the second reading strategy, we teach students to make predictions about upcoming events and to compare these with the actual outcomes depicted in the text. In this manner, we stimulate students to look ahead while reading and to monitor their expectations afterwards.

Concerning this strategy, it is important to notice that it is actually not so important that the prediction is correct; it is more crucial that children learn to read actively with foresight. Distinguishing main issues from side issues targets the skills of main idea identification and summarising. In *One Book for Two*, students more specifically learn to ask and answer *who*, *what*, *where*, *when* and *why* questions in reference to the text, and to restate the main ideas of successive paragraphs or of the complete text.

Monitoring and regulating the understanding of words and expressions is essential for understanding texts as well. Therefore, in *One Book for Two*, the focus for students is on identifying words or expressions that are not understood independently, and to discover the meaning by looking for a definition, a synonym or a description in the text—by using context clues or illustrations, by referring to a dictionary or computer or by enlisting someone's help.

On the basis of the fifth strategy, we encourage students to monitor and check their comprehension regularly during reading and to regulate understanding of difficult sentences or passages by rereading, adjusting reading speed and identifying the meaning of unfamiliar words or expressions.

By means of the sixth selected strategy, we point out that different text genres—each with their own characteristics—can be distinguished. In this respect, *One Book for Two* instructs students in classifying text genres (e.g. stories, informative texts, persuasive texts) and in adjusting reading behaviour to them.

The last strategy focuses on learning to summarise texts graphically by means of making a scheme. In particular, we focus on learning to draw sequence schemes (illustrating the order of events or steps in a text, e.g. a recipe, successive events in a story); cause–effect schemes (visualising causes and effects described in the text, e.g. a text on global warming); and classification schemes (illustrating different groups distinguished in the text, e.g. a text on the different groups of instruments). Schematising is a tool used to represent the main ideas of a text in a structured way, and can be important in the transition from learning to read to reading to learn.

In combination, the selected strategies can be used prior to, during or after reading. The strategies used before reading aim to optimally prepare the reader. Strategies used during reading are mainly aimed at monitoring and regulating comprehension and understanding. Finally, strategies applied after reading focus on evaluating the reading process and understanding. Consequently, the selected strategies cover the entire reading process, encouraging students to orientate towards the text and to plan, monitor and reflect on their reading behaviour and understanding, and to regulate when necessary in order to get a better grip on reading comprehension. Of course, other reading strategies that teachers find important and relevant can also easily fit into the *One Book for Two* project.

As to the *instructional strategies* used during the explicit instruction of the reading strategies, we encourage teachers to focus specifically on extensive modelling of the use of reading comprehension strategies through demonstrating and thinking aloud. Additionally, a gradual transfer from external regulation by the teacher to self-regulation of strategy use by the students is stimulated throughout *One Book for Two*.

The stepwise instruction for each reading strategy consists of the following phases:

■ During a *whole-class instructional presentation and explanation phase*, the teacher explicitly explains and models by thinking aloud why, how and when a specific strategy can be beneficial during reading, in order to enhance understanding. By thinking aloud the teacher externalises the strategic processes that usually occur internally.

■ During a *phase of practice characterised by teacher support and coaching*, the teacher puts the reading strategies into practice together with the students. This phase is characterised by student assignments, systematic and explicit scaffolding and coaching by the teacher to engage students in applying and reflecting upon the strategies, and subsequent whole-class discussions using multiple examples.

■ The last phase comprises of more *independent practice to internalise strategy use*. This more independent practice takes place in cross-age peer tutoring pairs, more extensively discussed underneath.

Reading strategy cards and texts

To support and structure the peer tutoring interaction, *One Book for Two* comprises of a *strategy assignment card* for each reading strategy. The cards offer structure and visual support on the different steps in applying the reading strategies and include questions students should ask themselves before, during or after reading. These questions are text-independent and consequently, the cards are applicable to different texts and, in most cases, to different text genres. Moreover, the cards offer the opportunity for students to formulate additional questions themselves, helping them practise self-questioning. The different strategy cards are used by the teachers when first modelling and explaining the strategies, and remain later for students' reference in the tutoring pairs. This encourages students to apply the strategies—and as they do, they experience the benefits of using reading strategies.

Furthermore, *One Book for Two* comprises of a *selection of texts* on which to practise the application of the strategies, including three phases of explicit reading strategies instruction. Fiction as well as nonfiction texts are included. These texts were not purposely written or adapted for *One Book for Two*, but were selected from children's literature. The selection of the texts was primarily based on the fact that they explicitly elicit the use of specific reading strategies; moreover, texts corresponding to the reading and interest level of the students were preferred.

Weekly cross-age peer tutoring sessions

In *One Book for Two*, weekly peer tutoring activities (of 50 minutes a week) are organised throughout the school year in order to systematise RSU. This rather intensive and weekly implementation is important for students to develop the application of the reading strategies and for solid integration and internalisation of the different strategies. In planning these peer tutoring activities, we advise schools and teachers to opt for a fixed schedule in the timetable throughout the school year, with the intention of structurally embedding peer tutoring in the curriculum and classroom organisation.

The peer tutoring activities in *One Book for Two* are cross-age by nature, referring to older students tutoring younger students. *One Book for Two* pairs fifth- and sixth-graders with second- and third-graders respectively. Peer tutoring activities are organised classwide, so all students in a class become a tutor or tutee and all pairs are working simultaneously. While second or third-graders (aged 7 to 9) read, fifth- or sixth-grade tutors (aged 10 to 12) are required to monitor their tutees' reading process and understanding. They need to keep track of where it goes wrong or when it becomes difficult; they intervene when necessary with an appropriate reading strategy; and they provide help to establish or guarantee comprehension. In this respect, they learn to use the reading strategies together with a younger child, while simultaneously learning to apply them themselves.

The weekly peer tutoring sessions are organised and structured as follows:

■ Prior to each tutoring session, the teachers give a short *briefing* to their respective students (tutors or tutees), pointing out the main ideas or focus for the upcoming peer tutoring session (e.g. the specific reading strategy to practise).

■ *Tutors pick up their tutees* in second or third grade and accompany them to their reading spot. In this respect, we recommend assigning a fixed place to each pair, so no time is lost seeking places each week. It is important that the tutor and tutee are sitting side-by-side, so both students can see the book or text equally well. We further advise the use of both classrooms (of the tutors and the tutees) for placing the reading pairs. It is even better to add an extra room (e.g. the hallway, the student restaurant, an empty classroom), so that the pairs are more dispersed and disturb each other as little as possible.

■ After taking their places, the pairs start *reading and interacting*. As mentioned above, during the peer tutoring sessions, the application of the explicitly taught reading strategies is practised independently by means of the reading strategy assignment cards.

■ Finally, each peer tutoring session ends with a short *reflection* in which students' experiences are discussed and combined with teachers' observations. This is especially necessary and relevant for tutors in order to optimise upcoming sessions, but can also be important for tutees as a way to share or ventilate their experiences.

Below, one of the teachers using *One Book for Two* describes the idea behind the reflection after the peer tutoring sessions:

At the end of each session, we reflect with the tutors present in our classroom at that moment. The purpose of this discussion is sharing difficulties and positive elements they experienced during Reading Together. We talk about strategy-related topics, such as 'What do you do if your tutee is reading fairly well, but is not able to predict how a story will continue?', but also about social skills, such as 'How do you deal with a tutee who is not cooperating as expected?' Together the tutors search for solutions or they confirm each other. They experience that errors are allowed. Sometimes they recognise themselves in their tutee or they experience how a tutee's behaviour can elicit certain reactions in themselves as a tutor, leading also to insight in teacher reactions.

(Teacher, fifth grade)

As to the organisation of the peer tutoring sessions, it should be mentioned that this approach lends itself perfectly to differentiation and individualisation—because of the composition of the reading pairs, the selection of the reading texts and books, and the fact that each reading pair can work at their own pace. One of the school leaders explicitly acknowledges this element as an added value of the programme:

Within the framework of our school policy, we are constantly striving for new opportunities to offer children appropriate and differentiated education. If we can foster the interaction and social relationships between the children simultaneously, that's even more promising. Therefore, it was a unique opportunity to participate in the research project regarding peer tutoring and reading comprehension. Especially the new instructional techniques, the cross-age tutoring and the guidance and support throughout the project was appealing. Meanwhile, we are working with *One Book for Two* for the third school year. The innovative project allows a differentiated approach, engaging all students, while receiving attuned instruction and support. No one has to leave the class or to join a separate ability group.

(School leader)

Preparing the tutors

An important element in the peer tutoring component of *One Book for Two* is the organisation of tutor preparation for all fifth- and sixth-grade tutors. This is important, since research shows that peer tutoring is less effective when no attention is paid to sound prior preparation of the tutors (Parr & Townsend, 2002). We therefore developed a series of lessons and materials to assist students in becoming a good tutor. These comprise of: instructions for role play by the teacher and the students; examples of appropriate behaviour to engage in while working with a partner; worksheets for the students; and an administration card, on which the tutors are expected to write down which texts they read with their tutees and which strategies and assignment cards they practise during the sessions. Verbal explanations, modelling, role plays, discussions and student practice with teacher feedback are part of the tutor preparation. The tutor preparation sessions are scheduled at the beginning of the programme and require seven 50-minute lessons.

During the preparatory sessions, tutors receive information on the goals and the structure of the peer tutoring project and they learn to know their tasks and responsibilities. More specifically, the preparatory sessions focus on how to show interest, how to start and close a peer tutoring session, how to provide constructive feedback, how and when to provide praise, and how to offer explanations and assistance without giving away the answer. Furthermore, tutors are reassured that they are not expected to know everything; they can make mistakes or struggle. However, it is important to communicate this to the tutee and to seek help—for example, from the teacher. Part of the preparation is also an acquaintance activity between the class of the tutors and the class of the tutees (e.g. by means of a joint excursion, a sports or games afternoon, a quiz, arts activities) and the first encounter of the reading pairs (e.g. by means of an interview between tutor and tutee, a library visit).

More specifically, the following are provided as preparatory sessions:

■ Lesson 1: I get to know the project.
■ Lesson 2: We meet second/third-graders. Who do I know already?
■ Lesson 3: With a good listening attitude I show interest.
■ Lesson 4: Who exactly is my reading buddy?
■ Lesson 5: How do I start the reading session with my tutee? How do I finish a reading session? How do I complete the reading assignment card?
■ Lesson 6: How and when can I give compliments? How do I correct errors? Can I, as a tutor, make mistakes?
■ Lesson 7: Understood! So I'm a good reading buddy! Tutor graduation.

Peer tutoring pairs composition

Children are assigned to fixed pairs by mutual agreement of both classroom teachers. At first, the composition of the pairs is based on children's reading ability, so that poor and good fifth- or sixth-grade readers (aged 10 to 12) are respectively paired with poor and good second- or third-grade readers (aged 7 to 9). In this respect, it can be ensured that a sufficiently large difference in reading skills is present in all reading pairs. Only in this case will tutors feel effectively able to help and guide the tutees assigned to them. Note, however, that a tutor's reading skills say nothing about his or her qualities as a tutor for a younger reading buddy. On the contrary, a poor reader can be an excellent tutor; for example, because he or she has experienced reading difficulties him- or herself and therefore understands the feelings and efforts of a struggling tutee better.

A second guideline for composing the reading pairs is the personality of the students. In this respect, a socially and emotionally sensitive tutor can best be linked to a balanced, stable tutee; while on the other hand, an emotionally sensitive tutee is best accompanied by a strong and sociable tutor.

In principle, the idea is that reading pairs work together during a complete school year. However, it is of course important to provide the possibility of changing the composition of pairs who are not functioning well. Moreover, our experience shows that varying the composition of all pairs (e.g. halfway through the school year) provides new oxygen to the project and fuels pupils' motivation. Note, however, that it is not beneficial to change pairs on a regular basis or too often. It is important that students receive the time to get to know each other well. Only in this way do tutors develop a sense of responsibility for their reading buddy; the tutees feel safe and a bond of trust between them is created.

Interweaving explicit instruction and practice in peer tutoring pairs

With regard to the succession of explicit instruction of the reading strategies by the teacher and the independent practice in peer tutoring sessions, we recommend 'interweaving'. This implies that each lesson—in which a new reading strategy is introduced—is followed by at least one peer tutoring session in which that strategy is practised, when reading a text chosen by the teacher from the selection in the *One Book for Two* material. Next, a number of tutoring sessions follow, in which this same strategy is practised when reading books or texts that students can choose autonomously.

In the long run, when multiple or all strategies are practised, students are not only expected to make their own choice of reading books, but also to make their own choice of strategies and, accordingly, assignment cards to work on. This is important in view of the integration and internalisation of the use of different strategies and the transfer to reading texts outside the peer tutoring activities and reading lessons.

Reading material

In addition to the selection of texts provided in the *One Book for Two* materials, we urge teachers to include tutoring sessions with books or texts that the pairs select themselves from the school or class library, on the basis of their own interests and preferences. In this respect, it is important that the chosen books or texts are just above tutees' readability level, since a tutor with a higher reading level will be guiding the tutee through the reading.

From our experiences with *One Book for Two*, it appears that the free selection of reading material is very popular. Children report reading to be more fun and interesting when they can pick books or other texts (e.g. children's magazines, newspapers) themselves, provided that a wide variety of attractive books and different text genres is present at school. In this respect, some of our pilot schools made an agreement with the local public library in order to ensure the supply of new and varied reading material on a regular basis.

As to the reading materials used during the peer tutoring sessions in *One Book for Two*, one of the teachers illustrates how they work as follows:

> Since we also want to encourage students' reading pleasure, we look for motivating reading stuff, in which children are encouraged to do something with the information from the text. In this respect, reading serves as a functional activity, as is also the case in daily life. For example, playing a board game together after reading an explanation of that game, collaborating on an artwork after reading about a painter's life, work and techniques. In this respect, the reading material also contains challenging tasks. During a school project on 'Safety on the way to school', for example, our pairs worked with a text regarding the parts of a safe bicycle (e.g. bell, reflectors, lights, brakes). Afterwards they developed a checklist based on the text and they used their checklist to perform a control on the bikes of the tutees, who were asked to bring these to school that day. Another time, the answers of an animal quiz were checked by means of informative articles about animals. As reading material we also use texts from our own manual, books students choose from the class and public library, and texts from children's magazines, newspapers.
>
> (Teacher, second grade)

Role of the teachers and schools

In *One Book for Two*, teachers play an important and active role during the peer tutoring activities. They take on a new role of monitor, coach and facilitator. More particularly, teachers are active participants who monitor progress and student interaction, provide corrective and instructional feedback, and praise their students. When necessary, teachers can: model good helping behaviour; give examples; reexplain the application of the reading strategies on the one hand, and tutor skills on the other; and observe whether targeted skills are being practised.

One teacher phrases her changing role in our programme as follows:

> During tutor reading, it is important that we are always present. In the beginning, it felt somewhat uncomfortable. When to intervene? Is it even desirable to intervene? Or is it enough just to be near? We especially learned we had to 'let go'. It is important to be present when children have questions. Closely observing and supporting here and there when students are floating off. Modelling for a short time—taking over the tutor role—to unravel the text more in-depth. However, we have to beware not to intervene too frequently by sliding back in the traditional teacher role. The children have to find out what is going wrong themselves and receive a lot of feedback and useful tips from their peers.
>
> (Teacher, second grade)

Based on our studies, teachers can be prepared effectively to implement *One Book for Two* in their daily teaching (Van Keer & Verhaeghe, 2005b). Adequate support and the development of a school-wide vision on reading comprehension promotion at the school level is recommendable, especially since developing into a proficient reader can only be the result of a long process throughout one's school career and various literacy experiences. Furthermore, it is necessary that teachers believe in the relevance of explicit reading strategy instruction and peer dialogue, and are willing to engage in regular cross-class meetings. Moreover, school leaders can be a catalyst in this respect by providing opportunities for teacher dialogue and observation of each other at work, and by planning the school year reading curriculum.

ONE BOOK FOR TWO
DOES IT WORK?

Explaining something in your own words to others is the best way to learn.

This is a statement we often hear from teachers who regularly engage their students in opportunities to collaborate and to articulate to their peers what they are learning. Research regarding the effectiveness of peer tutoring in general, and regarding *One Book for Two* in particular, confirm that these teachers indeed have it right. One-to-one attention offers opportunities which can hardly ever be realised in traditional whole-class instruction: extensive individualisation; immediate feedback; endorsement and error correction; increased engagement; and time-on-task.

In this chapter, we discuss the results of evaluations of *One Book for Two* in more detail. More particularly, we investigate two consecutive studies with second- and fifth-graders (Van Keer, 2004; Van Keer & Verhaeghe, 2005a) and a study with third-grade tutees (8 to 9 years) and sixth-grade cross-age tutors (11 to 12 years) (Van Keer & Vanderlinde, 2010). In these studies, the effectiveness of the combination of explicit instruction in reading strategies and peer tutoring is investigated by means of large-scale and quasi-experimental research designs. We more specifically report on the effectiveness of students' reading comprehension, reading fluency, reading strategy awareness and reading strategy use (RSU).

The evaluation studies were typified by the following characteristics:

- Participation of a relatively large number of students from different schools throughout Flanders
- Evaluation in authentic educational settings, by supporting teachers to introduce the innovative approach as part of the overall curriculum, in the regular classroom context and with the participation of all students during an entire school year
- Inclusion of a long-term follow-up of the students, six months after the close of the intervention
- Use of standardised reading comprehension tests instead of experimenter-designed tests
- Comparison of the added value of peer tutoring with teacher-led practice of RSU and comparison of the differential effectiveness of cross-age and reciprocal same-age peer tutoring within some studies.

Generally, the evaluation studies indicate that blending explicit reading strategy instruction with peer tutoring is successful in promoting both primary school tutors' and tutees' reading. The combination with cross-age peer tutoring activities is especially a promising approach to support students' gradually emerging literacy expertise, where students from different ages can benefit. In this respect, *One Book for Two* can be an answer for schools struggling with the search for an effective reading comprehension curriculum. Below, the design and the main results of the evaluation studies are discussed in more detail.

In addition to the effect studies, a process-oriented study will also be discussed. This study was set up to investigate and compare the dynamics and ongoing interaction processes in reciprocal same-age and cross-age peer tutoring pairs. The results of this study indicated significant differences favouring cross-age peer tutoring dyads with regard to the occurrence of interaction in general, and the incidence of different types of tutor questions and tutees seeking help in particular.

STUDIES IN SECOND AND FIFTH GRADE

Design of the studies

In second and fifth grade, two successive large-scale studies were performed (Van Keer, 2004; Van Keer & Verhaeghe, 2005a), both characterised by quasi-experimental research with a pretest/posttest-retention test control group design. In the first study, 444 second-grade (aged 7 to 8 years) and 454 fifth-grade (aged 10 to 11) students and their respective teachers from 44 classes in 25 different schools throughout Flanders took part. Participating teachers and their classes were assigned to four different research conditions or approaches regarding their reading comprehension instruction.

In the *strategies-only approach*, reading comprehension instruction was characterised by explicit instruction in reading strategies, followed by practice of these strategies in teacher-led whole-class settings. Furthermore, there were *same-age* and *cross-age peer tutoring approaches*, introducing identical explicit instruction in the same reading strategies; but the application of the reading strategies was respectively practised in reciprocal same-age pairs (i.e. second-graders tutoring other second-graders, and fifth-graders tutoring other fifth-graders) and cross-age pairs (fifth-graders tutoring second-grade tutees). The fourth condition in the study was a *traditional approach*, characterised by customary reading comprehension instruction without explicit reading strategies instruction, or peer tutoring or other types of peer-led interaction and discussion about text.

As to the approaches to reading comprehension instruction, all lessons and activities were conducted by the regular teachers and embedded in regular school time during periods allocated for reading instruction. The interventions were not supplementary to other reading comprehension classes taking place. Teachers applying the first three approaches of reading comprehension instruction were coached by the researchers to substitute their traditional way of teaching comprehension with one of the innovative approaches.

The second study with second- and fifth-graders is a partial replication of the first one, this time with 396 second-graders and 449 fifth-graders from 42 different classrooms. In this study, same-age and cross-age peer tutoring and a traditional approach were again implemented. The strategies-only approach was not included in this second study.

The instruments used in both studies were Dutch standardised tests, measuring students' reading comprehension achievement (Staphorsius & Krom, 1996; Verhoeven, 1993) and their decoding fluency (Brus, 1969). Furthermore, a self-report questionnaire with respect to the use of reading comprehension strategies before, during and after reading was also used (Van Keer & Verhaeghe, 2005a). The instruments were used on all three measurement occasions.

The pretest was carried out in October (second and fifth grade) before the initiation of the interventions; the posttest occurred in May and June (second and fifth grade) after the completion of the interventions; and the retention test took place in December in the following school year (when children were already in third and sixth grade). In accordance with the research plan and design, none of the third- and sixth-grade teachers pursued the strategies-only, same-age or cross-age peer tutoring approach. Consequently, between post- and retention test (i.e. in the first term of third and sixth grade) all students received traditional reading comprehension instruction, without explicit reading strategies instruction or peer tutoring.

Results regarding reading comprehension

The findings of both evaluation studies generally confirm prior research, underlining the educational benefits of explicit reading strategies instruction and peer-led interaction about texts for students' reading comprehension performance.

For *second-graders*, the results of the first study revealed significant effects at posttest for the strategies-only and the cross-age peer tutoring approaches. This implies that after being engaged in one of these approaches for reading comprehension instruction during a complete school year, second-grade students made significantly more progress in reading comprehension than children receiving traditional reading comprehension instruction. Also in the second study, the pre- to posttest change of second-graders in the cross-age peer tutoring approach was significantly better than that of students receiving the traditional approach (effect size 0.42).

With regard to the progress over the whole period from pretest to retention test, however, the differences between cross-age peer tutoring students and students in the traditional approach were no longer significant. In both studies, no significant effects were found for students in the same-age peer tutoring approach.

In sum, the results of both studies especially document the effectiveness of fostering reading comprehension by providing students with explicit instruction in reading strategies, followed by practice in cross-age peer tutoring activities led by a fifth-grade (aged 10 to 11) tutor. This highlights the higher potential of the cross-age peer tutoring approach.

More particularly, it can be hypothesised that the significant findings for second-graders can be attributed to two essential elements of the instructional approach: namely, the individualised practice and assistance provided to the second-graders; and the fact that fifth-graders appear to be sufficiently competent in offering this support regarding the use of reading strategies effectively. In the strategies-only and same-age approach, both essential prerequisites are not fulfilled simultaneously. The strategies-only approach is characterised by proficient support by the teacher, but no individualised attention is offered. On the other hand, the same-age peer tutoring approach supplies individualised assistance, but it can be assumed that second-graders are not able yet to supervise and tutor the practice of reading strategies effectively.

One of the teachers involved in the evaluation study refers to the added value of the cross-age peer tutoring approach as follows:

> The children adore reading together! They really look forward to the peer reading sessions. This cross-age form of collaboration and taking care of each other is a unique opportunity to foster reading and reading motivation, but it is also a fantastic tool to qualify students in social relationships. It stimulates their self-concept. The personal bond between tutor and tutee gives the collaboration an unconstrained and relaxed character. Among themselves, the children feel free to express their opinion or to ask questions. The tutees receive individual attention, we—as a teacher—cannot provide in this way and intensity.
>
> (Teacher, second grade)

Furthermore, the finding that no long-term effects were found in both studies confirms the idea that for these young primary school students, enduring effects are only likely to appear if the approach is continued in the next school year. Further longitudinal studies are needed to evaluate this hypothesis.

For *fifth-graders*, the results of the first study indicate significantly higher progress in students in the cross-age peer tutoring (effect size of 0.36) and strategies-only approaches (effect size of 0.31), in comparison with students receiving traditional reading comprehension instruction. What is interesting, however, is that students from these approaches also keep growing in the long term, resulting in significantly larger progress from pretest to retention test with effect sizes of 0.75 and 0.46 respectively. When comparing the cross-age and reciprocal same-age peer tutoring approach, the results also indicate significantly larger progress from pretest to retention test for cross-age peer tutoring students (effect size of 0.56).

As to the second study, students in both same-age and cross-age peer tutoring approaches appear to perform significantly better at posttest compared to their peers receiving a traditional reading comprehension approach (effect sizes of 0.21 and 0.28 respectively). In the long run, only students in the cross-age peer tutoring approach experienced significant learning gains (effect size of 0.42). In this respect, the results of the second study seem to confirm the findings of the first study, especially with respect to the positive short- and long-term effects of the cross-age peer tutoring approach.

In sum, the combination of both studies confirms that explicit reading strategies instruction, complemented with either teacher- or peer-mediated practice, fosters fifth-graders' reading comprehension performance more than traditional reading instruction. Moreover, except for students practising the reading strategies by alternating between the role of tutor and tutee in reciprocal same-age tutoring, the effectiveness of the innovative reading comprehension instruction is corroborated by the significant long-term effects at the retention test, six months after the end of the interventions.

Taking into account the magnitude of the posttest and retention test effects, fifth-graders especially appear to benefit the most from being engaged as tutors in the cross-age peer tutoring approach. These students' learning gains outperform other fifth-graders' growth—and they have the most persistent long-term progress in reading comprehension. This prominent result is also strongly recognised by teachers involved in the evaluation studies. One of the teachers in the cross-age peer tutoring approach formulates her experiences regarding the effectiveness in this way:

> [I]n September, I started from the idea that the project would do no harm. But now I am convinced that it really helped a great deal. Low-achieving readers boosted their reading skills in different areas: fluency, comprehension, reading self-confidence.

From this I conclude: Practice makes perfect! Moreover, high achievers also expanded their social and communication skills.

(Teacher, fifth grade)

A possible explanation for this positive effect of cross-age peer tutoring in particular relates to the nature of tutoring a peer in connection to using and acquiring reading strategies. Tutoring requires tutors to focus their attention on the tutee's reading, to monitor their reading process and understanding, and to foster understanding by having their tutees apply relevant, well-selected reading strategies. Not having to read themselves makes it easier for tutors to give full attention to these metacognitive skills—and this might be even easier when tutoring a younger student with a lower reading level. Consequently, practising reading strategies while operating as a tutor for a younger student appears to foster independent and appropriate application of these reading strategies, leading to a long-term improvement of reading comprehension achievement.

One of the fifth-grade teachers involved in the evaluation study expresses this line of reasoning as follows:

The older students also develop a better understanding of the reading strategies, since they must communicate and transfer this to the younger student. Moreover, they find their tutor role very pleasant, which improves their learning attitude.

(Teacher, fifth grade)

Results regarding reading fluency

Although the focus of the interventions in the studies was on reading *comprehension*, it can be assumed that the weekly reading practice shared with peers in regular peer tutoring sessions also fostered students' reading *fluency*. Therefore, this element was included in the evaluation studies as well. However, the reading fluency data were only collected for *second-graders*.

The findings of the first study revealed that compared to conventional reading instruction, students practising strategic reading in cross-age tutoring sessions led by a fifth-grader grew significantly more in reading fluency in the course of second grade (effect size of 0.37). The effects of reading in reciprocal same-age pairs displayed a similar, though not statistically significant, trend. The nonexistence of an analogous result for students in the strategies-only approach demonstrates that receiving explicit reading strategies instruction without extra opportunities to practise oral reading in peer tutoring pairs does not result in increased reading fluency skills.

Generally, the results confirm the positive impact on oral fluent reading through readings shared with peers. However, in our studies, only a significant effect for peer tutoring activities in reading led by an older fifth-grade tutor was found. This implies that reading with a peer of comparable ability is not likely to improve fluency as much as reading with a more able reader. This result also leads us to assume that the assistance and corrective feedback provided by fifth-graders is more appropriate than the assistance and feedback given by second-grade peers aged from 7 to 8 years. Unfortunately, however, contrary to the positive results of the first study, the second study does not confirm the positive findings on students' reading fluency.

In addition to the standardised reading fluency test, evidence from teacher interviews also refer to the effectiveness of the cross-age peer tutoring approach on students' growth in fluency:

Each student is making progress, both in terms of decoding and reading fluency and at the level of reading comprehension.

(Teacher, second grade)

Results regarding RSU

In order to attempt to capture students' RSU, both second- and fifth-graders completed a self-report questionnaire at pretest, posttest and retention test. Only for *second-graders* were significant intervention effects found. More particularly, the results indicated that explicit reading strategies instruction followed by regular teacher- or peer-mediated practice enhanced second-graders' RSU significantly more than traditional reading comprehension instruction at the end of second grade.

In this regard, the first study shows effect sizes of 0.39, 0.45 and 0.33, respectively, for students in the same-age peer tutoring approach, the cross-age peer tutoring approach and the strategies-only approach. In the second study, effect sizes are 0.42 for the same-age peer tutoring approach and 0.71 for the cross-age peer tutoring approach. Only in the second study, and for students in the latter approach, did the difference remain significant at retention test (effect size of 0.62) compared to students receiving the traditional reading approach.

Moreover, the results of the second study also revealed a significant difference between the same-age and cross-age peer tutoring approach: both at post- and retention test, a significantly larger increase in the use of reading strategies was reported by second-graders in the cross-age peer tutoring approach (effect sizes of 0.29 at posttest and 0.31 at retention test).

To summarise, over the two studies, the second-grade results imply that by receiving explicit strategy instruction and practice, second-graders start to use reading strategies more during the reading process to enhance the likeliness of comprehension. When comparing the magnitude and the maintenance of the effects, fifth-graders functioning as tutors for second-graders in cross-age pairs appear to be the most effective in realising this, even in the long term.

Unfortunately, in contrast to the second-grade results, no significant results were found for *fifth-graders'* reports of RSU. It is thought that this finding might be due to a higher inclination towards social desirability in fifth-graders when completing the questionnaire. However, further research is necessary in this respect, combining (for example) self-report questionnaires with reading strategy tests, thinking-aloud tasks or stimulated recall interviews, to shed light on students' actual reading behaviour and their application of reading strategies.

Future studies in this respect will indeed be relevant, since in interviews, fifth-graders— in the cross-age peer tutoring approach especially—explicitly attributed their progress in the use of reading strategies to the performance of their tutor role:

Now I know better how to read for understanding. Before I became a tutor, I never really thought about things, such as 'What will the text be about? What to expect?' So that was difficult. But with peer tutoring, you learn that you have to look at the title and the pictures first and to think about the remainder of the text. Then you start reading and after a first part you think about whether you understand everything, and you tell yourself in your own words what you read and what might follow. I think this helps to understand texts. Moreover, asking this kind of question also helps my reading buddy from second grade.

(Student, fifth grade)

I actually have problems myself with reading comprehension. But through peer tutoring it is a bit easier for me now, because I had to teach my tutee how to deal with and understand texts. So now it goes better for me as well. I have learned to ask questions, to reread when I don't understand something, or to read somewhat further or look at the accompanying pictures in order to find an explanation for a difficult word.

(Student, fifth grade)

STUDY IN THIRD AND SIXTH GRADE

Design of the study

Following the studies in second and fifth grade, the study in third and sixth grade (Van Keer & Vanderlinde, 2010) was characterised by a quasi-experimental design as well. In this study, however, no retention test was included and a pretest/posttest design was used. In total, 21 third-grade and 18 sixth-grade teachers and their respective 405 and 357 students from 15 different schools throughout Flanders took part. Participating teachers and their classes were assigned to two research conditions or reading comprehension approaches.

The experimental condition or cross-age peer tutoring approach used *One Book for Two* with sixth-graders (aged 11 to 12) functioning as cross-age tutors for third-grade (aged 8 to 9) tutees (see Chapter 6); while in the control condition, teachers used their traditional approach, characterised by customary reading comprehension instruction without explicit reading strategies instruction, peer tutoring or other types of peer-led interaction and discussion about text. Analogous with the above mentioned studies, all *One Book for Two* activities in the experimental condition were performed by the classroom teachers and embedded in regular school time during periods allocated for reading instruction. Again, the experimental intervention was implemented during an entire school year.

Standardised tests were used to measure students' reading comprehension performance (Staphorsius & Krom, 1996) and students completed two self-report questionnaires: the Index of Reading Awareness (Jacobs & Paris, 1987) and the RSU scale (Pereira-Laird & Deane, 1997). The former more particularly focuses on students' awareness of the importance of conditional knowledge (i.e. children's understanding of when and why particular reading strategies should be applied), planning ahead for specific purposes, regulation of the reading process by monitoring progress and by using fix-up strategies as needed, and evaluation of task, goals and personal skills. The RSU scale distinguishes between cognitive RSU (i.e. rehearsal, organisation and elaboration strategies) and metacognitive RSU (i.e. planning, monitoring and regulation strategies).

Results regarding reading strategy awareness and use

As to students' reading strategy awareness, the results revealed that third-grade tutees reported significantly more overall strategy awareness and, in particular, awareness of the surplus value of regulating their reading process by monitoring and applying reading strategies, compared to third-graders receiving traditional reading comprehension instruction. For sixth-grade tutors, a significant impact of cross-age peer tutoring was found on their awareness of the importance of evaluating reading tasks, goals and personal reading skills.

The results regarding students' reported use of cognitive and metacognitive reading strategies indicate that at posttest, both third-grade tutees and sixth-grade tutors outperformed their peers receiving traditional reading comprehension instruction with regard to their overall reported strategy use. Moreover, sixth-grade tutors also significantly outperformed control group students as to the reported use of metacognitive reading strategies in particular. The stronger results for sixth-graders with regard to reported overall strategy use, and the more limited impact on only one subscale of strategy awareness, led us to suspect that reading instruction in both the experimental and control group classes enabled the emerging awareness of the relevance of reading strategies; while the application of these strategies appears to be promoted by being additionally engaged in the cross-age peer tutoring approach.

As to the above mentioned effectiveness of the experimental condition for both reading strategy awareness and use, the results revealed no differential effects for high- and low-achieving readers. This implies that all students, irrespective of their achievement level, gained as much from receiving explicit instruction in reading strategies, followed by practice in cross-age peer tutoring pairs.

Results regarding reading comprehension

In contrast to the aforementioned studies in second and fifth grade, the results for third and sixth grade (ages 8 to 9 and 11 to 12) revealed no significant effects of engaging students in the blend of explicit reading strategy instruction and cross-age peer tutoring. Consequently, it appeared that the promotion of students' reading strategy awareness and use did not yield significantly better comprehension performance. This result might be due to the fact that the intervention in the third- and sixth-grade study lasted somewhat shorter. However, more in-depth research in this respect is necessary.

PROCESS-ORIENTED STUDY OF INTERACTION IN PEER TUTORING READING GROUPS

Design of the study

Taking into account the benefits to tutors and tutees in cross-age peer tutoring, a video-based analysis was performed on the interactions during cross-age and reciprocal same-age peer tutoring, to explore whether the interaction in cross-age peer tutoring could be characterised as more beneficial for learning than the reciprocal same-age peer tutoring interaction. More specifically, the complete interaction of 18 second- and fifth-grade peer tutoring pairs was videotaped during four to five tutoring sessions (i.e. eight cross-age pairs; six same-age second-grade pairs; four same-age fifth-grade pairs). The video data were collected within the context of the first study with second- and fifth-grade students.

To analyse students' interaction during peer tutoring, a coding system was developed, distinguishing the following broad dimensions: administration, reading, completing assignment cards, interaction and off-task behaviour. Given the importance of—and the specific focus on—peer interaction, this dimension was further subdivided into affective, regulative (i.e. planning, monitoring and evaluation of the assignment and the reading process) and cognitive interaction (i.e. tutor questions, tutee answers, tutee mistakes and seeking help, tutor help, tutees accepting or questioning help, tutee self-corrections and comments upon the content or the structure of the texts).

Results

The results indicated that the vast majority of the time spent in the peer tutoring sessions was devoted to reading. Almost no time was spent off-task, which confirmed the hypothesised high time-on-task during peer tutoring activities. On average, one-fifth of the sessions was spent on interaction between partners, predominantly characterised by tutor questions, tutees' responses to these questions, tutors providing help and students commenting upon the text. To a lesser extent, the discourse was typified by tutees asking for help, accepting or questioning help and correcting their own mistakes.

As to tutor questions, it appeared that the interaction was primarily organised around spontaneous thinking questions: asking tutees to go beyond the explicit material and to make connections among ideas. As to the help provided by the tutors, almost no mistakes or questions for help were ignored. Moreover, the help tutors offered could be regarded as of highly quality, including high-level explanation.

With regard to the differences between same-age and cross-age peer tutoring, the results revealed differences in the amount of time students were engaged in interaction, with cross-age pairs interacting significantly more. In particular, fifth-grade (aged 10 to 11) cross-age tutors raised significantly more spontaneous questions of all kinds (i.e. thinking, probing, hint and metacognitive questions). Second-grade (aged 7 to 8) cross-age tutees asked significantly more review, thinking and metacognitive questions during help seeking than their same-age peers. In this respect, it can be assumed that cross-age tutors considered themselves as experts in comparison with their younger tutees, which appealed to their sense of responsibility to check tutees' comprehension thoroughly. Likewise, it appears that cross-age tutees felt more confident in asking for help from fifth-graders because of their age and achievement gap.

CONCLUSION

Taking into account the above research and findings on reading comprehension, fluency and reading strategy awareness and use, it appears that introducing explicit instruction in reading strategies in the reading comprehension curriculum is important. In addition, the studies overall revealed the significance of combining this explicit reading strategy instruction with regular practice in peer tutoring pairs, and cross-age peer tutoring in particular, as operationalised in *One Book for Two* (see Chapter 6). Cross-age tutoring appears to be the most favourable for both tutees and tutors, and also in the long-term.

The strong presence of high-quality interaction between the cross-age peers, characterised by a wide range of different high-level questions and well-elaborated responses, can be regarded as underlying these findings. Both parties benefit from the interactive relationship and the effect sizes even suggest that the positive effect of cross-age peer tutoring is larger for the tutor than for the tutees. 'To tutor is to learn twice'—so it actually seems! A possible explanation of this result may lie in the fact that the tutors are challenged to reflect on the learning content more thoroughly, in depth and from different perspectives. Consequently, tutors develop a better understanding and take their knowledge and skills to a higher level. Moreover, it appears that the *One Book for Two* approach works equally well for low, average and high achievers.

Further research is still necessary to evaluate the effectiveness in a larger variety of (international) contexts. It should also be acknowledged that owing to the complexity of the innovative approaches, we are not able to draw conclusions about the relative contribution of the different constituent components in the approach (e.g. the focus on the integrated teaching and acquisition of a series of different strategies; the instructional approach focusing on explicit teacher explanations; modelling and a gradual transfer from teacher to student regulation; the regular opportunities to practise strategic reading). We hypothesise that it is the combination of these different elements that contributes to the positive effects found. However, this is only an assumption and an issue for future research.

8 READING IN PAIRS

WHAT IS IT?

This chapter presents *Reading in Pairs*, a programme based on peer tutoring—with family involvement—for reading improvement. This programme, with materials published in Catalan, Spanish, Basque and English, is being developed by more than 200 schools, organised in networks. Throughout these pages, their conceptual bases are reviewed and their characteristics described. This programme opts for a highly structured organisation between tutor and tutee, with activity sheets for the joint activity, in which control is progressively transferred to the pairs.

INTRODUCTION

In order to offer tools to schools and teachers to enhance their students' reading competence, the Research Group on Peer Learning (GRAI), from the Universitat Autònoma de Barcelona (Catalonia), has promoted the educational programme *Llegim en Parella* or *Reading in Pairs*.

Reading in Pairs combines peer tutoring and family involvement. Its activities (reading and reading comprehension in pairs) are supported by an activity sheet and by a highly structured interaction at the beginning of the programme, which—when pairs have become familiarised with them—allow a more progressive and creative use.

Reading in Pairs is the result of research and school practice that members of the GRAI have developed from international experiences (especially Read On—Topping & Hogan, 1999), our own previous work (Duran, 2007; Duran & Flores, 2008; Valdebenito & Duran, 2010) and a pilot study (Duran & Oller, 2006; Duran, Oller & Utset, 2007), which gave rise to the creation of networks of centres in Catalonia, the Basque country, Spain and Chile. At present, there are about 200 primary and secondary schools that use the programme in Spanish, Catalan, Basque and English. Materials are published in Spanish (Duran, Blanch, Corcelles, Fernández et al., 2011a), Basque (Duran, Blanch, Corcelles, Flores et al., 2011b) and Catalan (Duran et al., 2013).

Implementing the programme with all these centres, teachers, students and families has allowed us to research and reflect with them. Thanks to their involvement and enthusiasm, we have had the opportunity to improve and develop *Reading in Pairs*, so we believe that it can be presented not as something theoretical, designed at the University, but as a result of a practical dialogue.

CONCEPTUAL BASIS

In this section, we review the three conceptual elements on which rest the *Reading in Pairs* programme—peer tutoring, family involvement and reading—basing them on psycho-pedagogical research and educational knowledge.

Peer tutoring

As we have seen in the first part of the book, properly structured interaction between students is a powerful engine for significant learning. Through an interaction that is structured by the teacher, the students offer pedagogical aids to each other and are immersed in interactions that allow for customisation and adjustment of actions, placed in small groups or in pairs. Learning to cooperate is also functional learning, because it is a key competence for the democratic society of knowledge (Ritchen & Salvanik, 2003).

In *Reading in Pairs*, peer tutoring is understood as a peer learning method based on the creation of pairs of students with an asymmetrical relationship (derived from the adoption of the role of tutor and tutee, respectively) and a common objective, known and shared (for example, the acquisition of curricular skills), which is achieved through a relationship framework planned by the teacher (Duran & Vidal, 2004).

While there are many school practices based on peer tutoring, in the Spanish speakers' context recently, we can also find more experiences each day of the uses of tutoring in compulsory education. Materials have been designed that focus on the teaching and learning of Catalan (Duran, Torró & Vilar, 2003) and Spanish (Duran & Vidal, 2004), to help to introduce peer tutoring as a methodological option that enriches the range of resources in schools. The multiple and varied experiences which have been derived from here (Duran, 2006) allow us to see that it is not only tutees who learn through permanent and personalised support received from peer tutors—but that tutors also learn, because teaching can be a good way of learning (Duran, 2014).

Family involvement in school activities

The second component of the programme focuses on family support in reading carried out in the home. In recent decades, scientific literature has supported the positive influence that the active involvement of the families has on the school success of their sons and daughters (J. Lam, Cheung & R. Lam, 2009; Powell, Son, File & San Juan, 2010). Studies in different geographical contexts (Martínez, 1992; Nailing, 2010; Ofsted, 2001) conclude that when families participate and collaborate actively with the school, their children increase in academic performance and, in addition, the school improves its quality of teaching.

But, as we all know, to facilitate family participation is not an easy task. In this sense, it seems urgent to provide resources to families through strategies for the stimulation and support of their children in learning and education, with the aim of favouring the creation of family environments that promote the development of positive attitudes towards learning and the generation of expectations for school success (Martínez, 2004). Within this range of possibilities, one is that families support their children's learning from home and thereby, parents share in some way the role of teacher (Oliva & Palacios, 1998). In this context, Wolfendale and Topping (1996) collected studies that demonstrated the positive influence on school performance that the collaboration of members of the family (parents, grandparents or siblings) had when learning from home.

Other studies, such as that by Dearing, McCartney, Weiss and Simpkins (2004), or the *Progress in International Reading Literacy Study* report (Mullis, Martin, Foy & Drucker, 2012), demonstrate the benefits that family participation have in improving students' reading comprehension. To facilitate collaboration between teachers and families it is important that schools give parents guidelines for teaching to read, and encourage and support them to be effective (Al-Momani, Ihmeideh & Naba'h, 2010). Supporting this need and other similar practices with good results, such as the Read On programme or family tutoring in mathematics (Topping & Bamford, 1998), *Reading in Pairs* aims to educate families to act as their sons or daughters' reading tutors at home.

Reading competence

Reading competence includes a set of knowledge, skills and strategies that is built throughout life in different contexts and communities, in which the individual participates and takes a leading role, reflecting and interpreting the meaning of the text. It can be defined as the ability to understand and use written texts and reflect and engage personally with them, in order to achieve personal objectives, develop personal knowledge and potential and participate in society (OECD, 2009).

From the perspective of *Reading in Pairs*, the development of reading requires an active role from the reader and deliberate teaching with a teacher or a more competent reader, involving the entire school (and the educative community). This perspective holds that, except for very specific situations (such as when reading a phone number or an address), reading involves understanding the written text. Reading comprehension is located at the core of reading.

What are the strategies to teach students to learn how to understand texts? According to Solé (1992), the reader should know his or her reading purposes; activate and bring prior relevant knowledge to the content of the text; focus on the essential information; assess the consistency between the content of the text and previous knowledge; adopt an interactive and critical role; check text understanding, based on recapitulation and self-questioning; and finally, make inferences, interpretations, assumptions or predictions and conclusions.

Research tells us that silent reading, by itself, does not improve reading comprehension, but that what is decisive is the aid received to understand (Block et al., 2009). As Jiménez and O'Shanahan (2008) assert, formal and explicit instruction in reading strategies tends to improve reading comprehension. Monitoring comprehension (consciousness of one's own processes of understanding), cooperative learning (joint learning of reading strategies) and formulation of questions with immediate feedback are some of the most effective strategies for understanding texts.

Following these recommendations, *Reading in Pairs* attempts to create real reading situations. Through the activity sheets, which will be discussed later, students deal with texts from their actual environment, selected on the basis of a variety of formats and adequacy of complexity and meaning. The activity sheet generates a structure of interaction with three moments:

1   Before reading, there are questions that help to explore the characteristics of the text, formulate hypotheses or predictions of content and activate prior knowledge.
2   During reading, the tutor and tutee follow a sequence of reading aloud and use a particular PR technique.

3   Finally, after reading, different formats of questions or activities on reading comprehension are asked, which promote reflection on initial assumptions and the difficulties that have arisen and facilitate the identification of the main ideas, the intention of
the author and the discovery of the lexicon.

At the end, activity sheets that guide the interaction of pairs provide some complementary
or joint activities, as well as encouraging an expressive reading of the text, with adjustments in intonation, appropriation and enrichments—which are characteristic of having
succeeded in a deep level of understanding.

This type of shared reading or partner activity also facilitates the development of oral
skills, to create communicative situations in which students learn to reflect on the use of
the language (Vilà, 2002). This is particularly important in the learning of a foreign language. Oral exchanges that occur within pairs, with the structure of interaction facilitated
by teachers, promote reasoning and practice of communication strategies and language
resources, as well as the development of active and cooperative listening.

Finally, we would like to insist on the idea that reading is not a technique that can
be learned all at once (Solé, 2005). Reading competence, as with other competences,
supports increasing degrees of deepening understanding. For this reason, reading, and
especially reading comprehension, has to be taught along with scholarship. Schools use
Reading in Pairs at all levels of primary education, with required adjustments.

OBJECTIVES AND COMPETENCES
OF *READING IN PAIRS*

Reading in Pairs is a set of materials that make up an educational programme that
uses peer tutoring—in the school between students, and at home between students and
relatives—for the improvement of reading and reading comprehension. These materials
help schools, through the adjustment of interests and adaptation to their own contexts, in
the achievement of the following objectives:

■   Putting within reach teachers' inclusively oriented methodologies. Peer learning, and
peer tutoring in particular, allows living diversity as a positive value: it is the difference (in this case between tutor and tutee) by which we learn.

■   Developing new forms for language teaching. Peer tutoring and family support can
complement the performances of teaching and learning language skills that commonly occur in our classrooms, building spaces for personalised aid with high levels
of oral interaction in schools, but also at home.

■   Improving the reading competence, and especially reading comprehension, of students. This systematic use of comprehension strategies can help to achieve the challenge noted in the latest PISA report—that all students must reach a sufficient level
of reading ability for lifelong learning (OECD, 2014).

■   Fostering cooperation among students. Cooperation is a key competence in today's
knowledge society and is, in itself, a valuable competence that develops social skills
and basic attitudes for democratic life.

■   Promoting the involvement of families in school activities and increasing the range
of opportunities for participation. After a brief training session, parents have the possibility to tutor their sons or daughters in reading at home.

We will now present the contribution of the programme to the achievement of some basic skills and the development of reading.

Contributions of *Reading in Pairs* to basic competences

As mentioned previously, one of the main objectives of *Reading in Pairs* is to improve reading competence, a basic and transversal competence, since it is necessary for learning in all curricular areas. For this reason, the programme promotes these spaces for reading, both at school and at home, helping to consolidate the habit of reading as a basic tool for the exercise of the right to education and to culture in the context of the knowledge society. This contributes to the development of the following core competences.

Learning to learn competence

Learning to learn means having abilities to engage in learning and be able to continue learning more effectively and autonomously, according to one's own objectives and needs. In *Reading in Pairs*, the regular activity of self-assessment in pairs allows reflection by self-regulated learning. In this way, students will become aware of their own abilities, of the processes of work carried out and the strategies needed to learn, to become increasingly effective and autonomous in learning. All these processes contribute to the feeling of personal competence that has a direct impact on motivation and confidence in oneself and in one's taste for learning.

Linguistic communication competence

People build their thinking through interactions with others. Learning is a social activity that requires good communication for significant understanding of new information and construction of increasingly more elaborate knowledge networks. This competence refers to the use of language as an instrument of oral and written communication, representation, interpretation and understanding of reality; construction and communication of knowledge, and organisation and self-regulation of thought, emotion and behaviour. *Reading in Pairs* is based on communication between students (tutor and tutee) or between student and family, and on learning from interaction.

Information handling and digital competence

Students need skills to seek, obtain, process and communicate information and to transform it into knowledge, embodying different abilities, ranging from information access to its transmission through various supports. Activity sheets may promote the development of methodologies that foster autonomy, efficiency, responsibility, criticality and a reflective spirit in the selection, treatment and use of the information in different media and technologies.

Social and civic competence

Cooperation and coexistence are key elements to build a democratic society with citizens committed to social improvement. This competence is made up from diverse knowledge and complex skills that allow participation, decision-making, choosing how to behave in certain situations and taking responsibility for personal elections. All these processes take place in the pair.

Autonomy and personal initiative competence

Through this competence, ideas can be transformed into actions; objectives proposed and plans made to carry them out. It requires reworking previous approaches or developing new ideas, finding solutions and putting them into practice. The programme promotes the acquisition of the consciousness of responsibility towards the proposed task: perseverance, self-knowledge and self-esteem; creativity, self-criticism and emotional control; and the ability to choose activities that are needed to improve the objectives of work and time management, as well as the ability to meet the challenges and learn from mistakes.

DESCRIPTION OF *READING IN PAIRS*

As in any educational project, the success of the programme is strongly linked to the enthusiasm that can emerge between its protagonists. In this sense, it is essential that involved teachers and the school in general see *Reading in Pairs* in a positive way. It is because the students are different—with different levels of reading ability—that they will learn. Through peer tutoring, students and the school community have the possibility to view how diversity, far from being a problem, arises as a positive element for the pedagogical task.

It is also important that peer tutors understand this opportunity, to get under the skin of 'a teacher', as a very interesting experience and, above all, a good learning opportunity. For tutee students, it will also invite them to use personalised aid from the tutors—a true luxury in the school context—in a framework where not only do they learn, but also do the tutors who are teaching them.

It is a really interesting challenge to be able to reach families who can take more advantage of the programme, to encourage them to create these small familiar spaces where, in addition to providing direct support to the schooling of their children, they will have the opportunity to establish a relationship of trust. It should be encouraging to families—especially to those who are in most need of the programme—that, with the support of the school, they will be able to do perfectly well as their children's reading tutors.

Pairing students

Even though in some cases it is possible to create pairs during previous training, it will usually be teachers who will determine student pairs, as a first step of the programme. Although the criteria for the establishment of pairs should be adjusted to the context of the school, we will discuss some guidelines.

If we choose a *cross-age tutoring* format, with students of different ages or courses, the studies reviewed recommend that the difference in knowledge or competences between tutor and tutee should not to be too large. Our experience would suggest that, if you opt for pairs of students in different years, tutors should be two years older—no more.

Where pairs are matched using ratings of student performance in the language area (which could be an easy way for teachers), or where matching is done based on the results of a test of linguistic competence, it is necessary to promote a similar 'distance' between tutor and tutee along the set of pairs. This means ensuring that more able tutors are matched with more able tutees; that is, the tutors with the best marks are matched with the tutee with the best marks, and so on.

If we opt for *same-age tutoring*, we order the students according to linguistic ability within the class group, dividing the ranked list into two in the middle and matching the most able tutor with the most able tutee. In addition, with students on the same course, there is the possibility of creating reciprocal peer tutoring, where tutor and tutee alternate roles in each session or every week. In this form, reciprocal tutoring requires matching pairs in such a way that the partners have a similar level of competence.

Finally, whether adopting same- or cross-age tutoring, fixed or reciprocal, you need to consider whether there will be changes in the pairs. We refer to a general change, not to individual cases requiring a change for some particular reason. In cases of such latter changes in pairs, we suggest you make only one and ask tutors to pass a detailed report on their tutees' progress to the new tutees. A brief report could also be asked from the tutees. However, we must not forget that success in peer tutoring requires that students have time to learn how to develop their role, adjusted to the characteristics of their peers. That is why we rather advise caution in deciding changes in pairs and, instead, give the students enough time to learn to work with their partners.

Regarding the creation of pairs in the family context, we would like to raise a couple of suggestions. First, schools must deploy a creative effort to publicise the programme and its benefits to the families, but especially for those families where involvement may be most useful to them. Logically, these will not be families who already stimulate children with cultural and educational events (for surely, they will be the first to show interest). It would be useful to reach families who need to establish spaces for educational dialogue and who have sometimes expressed their difficulties in doing so.

In terms of finding more appropriate ways to publicise the programme, it is worth asking about the use of cards (by mail or through the children); sending personal invitations (verbally); displaying posters in school; writing in the school newsletter or in the local press, and so on. Also, consider using personal supports—such as, for example, your own students (getting them to encourage their parents to participate); or through social workers visiting families where ordinary information tends not to arrive. When the school has implemented the programme, teachers can ask the families who participated in previous versions to encourage new families to take part. By showing that students in the school can also perform in the role of tutors can encourage the less predisposed family members to feel able to act as reading tutors.

To encourage families to participate in the programme, schools need to establish initial forms of support and assistance. A good decision is to appoint a coordinator of the programme who can establish a good level of communication and closeness with the families, and who can meet the doubts and questions that arise in the start-up.

Finally, we should understand family tutoring in a broad perspective: family tutors can be mothers or fathers; grandfathers or grandmothers; brothers or sisters; other relatives (cousins, uncles or aunts); or family support staff. Even if there are families where it seems impossible to undertake family tutoring, we should provide opportunities to participate after school with suitably trained volunteer staff.

Training for students and families

Research on peer tutoring has proven that the more structured the interaction between tutor and tutee, and the more closed the script that regulates what each pair member has to do, the better are the results (Cohen, et al., 1982; Topping & Ehly, 1998). Aware of this, *Reading in Pairs* opts for a highly structured framework of relations between tutor and tutee which ensures that, at all times, both members of the pair know what to do.

The option for a structured framework has this marked advantage, but requires at the same time a greater investment in training for the pair members. Before starting work in pairs, it is necessary to devote some sessions to the development of the respective roles. These sessions constitute an essential investment.

If students know enough about each other, and we already know who will be tutor and who will be tutee, it would be convenient to create pairs before starting prior training. If this is not so (say, if the group of tutors and tutees come from different courses), we will need to postpone the creation of pairs until the end of the training. In these training sessions, it is preferable to place tutors and tutees together, in order to put into practice what is explained.

Teachers have to determine the number of initial training sessions, depending on the students' characteristics. Our experience tells us that three sessions may be sufficient. In any case, the objectives of these sessions are:

1   Knowing the bases of the peer tutoring; understanding the learning of both roles; providing tips for tutors;
2   Learning the activities that structure the sessions and practising those that are necessary; learning prior to reading activities and simultaneous reading; using the 'Pause, Prompt and Praise' (PPP) technique; reading comprehension activities; expressive reading;
3   Familiarisation with support materials (e.g. activity sheets, language support, self-assessment guidelines);
4   Meeting the partner (especially if the pairs first meet after the initial training).

Regarding the training of families willing to participate in the programme, it may be more convenient to do this in one session, with all family members together. This session would include a brief presentation of the programme, modelling the activities and explaining support materials. It should ensure that, at the end of the session, family members feel safe with respect to participation in the programme and have the date of a follow-up meeting to assess performance.

Activities in tutoring sessions

After prior student and family training, peer tutoring sessions can start. Even though schools can take other decisions, *Reading in Pairs* opts for two 30-minute sessions per week during a term. In these sessions, the pairs sit together, side-by-side. It is advisable that the tutor is situated to the tutee's left (except if left-handed), to more easily monitor the activities. In order to avoid interfering with other pairs, especially at the time of reading aloud, it should be suggested that pair members sit closely together, raising their voices as little as possible. When tutoring takes place in the family context, the use of a comfortable space, with good light and minimum possible distraction is recommended.

Figure 8.1 represents the activities in the 30-minute session. We must insist once again on the importance of a clear structure that allows tutor and tutee to know what to do at all times. During the first sessions, this structure takes a rigid format, as if it were a fixed routine. Once the pair members have learned to perform the tasks derived from their respective roles, the control of the activity will be gradually transferred, encouraging a more free and creative use, as we will explain later.

At the beginning of the session, the teacher will distribute the activity sheet (which contains a brief text) and some reading comprehension activities. An example is provided in Figure 8.2. Usually, the activity sheet is distributed among tutees, because tutors receive them in a previous class in order to prepare them. When the programme is used for the learning of a foreign language, a sound file with the text read by a native speaker is provided. In some cases, especially with tutors with more difficulties, we can also provide additional support and response guidelines.

In the first 15 minutes, the activity revolves around reading. At first, the pair is requested to explore the characteristics of the text (format, title, structure, source, etc.); make a hypothesis or a prediction of the content; and think what they know and what they do not know regarding the content (anticipating potential problems that can be found). In short, the pairs activate their prior knowledge on the topic.

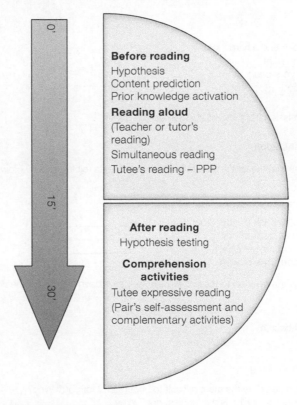

■ **Figure 8.1** Activities clock for session

A BARREL OF FUN

Before reading . . .

If you take a quick look at the text and the title, do you think you are going to enjoy it? Why? In your opinion, what type of text are you going to read: a story, a comic, a poem, or none of these? Why do you think so?

Tongue twister

Peter Piper picked a peck of pickled peppers,
A peck of pickled peppers Peter Piper picked.
If Peter Piper picked a peck of pickled peppers,
Where's the peck of pickled peppers Peter Piper picked?

Riddles

1   What has a neck and no head?
2   Which letter of the alphabet has the most water?
3   What has to be broken before you can use it?
4   Which month has 28 days?
5   What has a face and two hands but no arms or legs?
6   Why can't a man living in New York be buried in Chicago?

Idioms

1   Between a rock and a hard place
2   All in the same boat
3   The ball is in your court
4   Knock on wood

Adapted with permission from www.funenglishgames.com

Reading comprehension

1   Did you guess that the text is about different kind of texts related to fun? How could you guess it?

2   Decide if these sentences are True or False:

    a)   The peppers are in Peter's hand.   _____
    b)   Peter has a peck of nuts.   _____
    c)   Peter's surname is Wilson.   _____
    d)   The peppers are pickled.   _____

3   Did you guess the solution to the riddles? Try to match each riddle with the right solution.

    The C
    The clock
    All of them of course
    A bottle
    The egg
    Because he's still living

4   Which of these riddles is the most difficult to understand for you? Why?
5   And, in your opinion, which is the funniest one? Why?
6   Try to explain the meaning, with your own words, of the idioms above.
7   Choose one of the idioms related to your personal experience and explain the situation.

Extra activities

1   Try to learn by heart the tongue twister.
2   Make up a couple of riddles.

■ **Figure 8.2** Example of activity sheet

Only in the first sessions, or when students work with a very complex text, can the teacher or tutor first read aloud the text, acting as a model (that is why it is presented in parentheses in Figure 8.1). Both students then read aloud the text and the tutor checks the speed, pronunciation and intonation. Then, the tutee reads alone and the tutor applies the PPP technique (Wheldall & Colmar, 1990).

In this technique, the tutor notes when the tutee makes an error and waits a few seconds so that he or she may correct it; if it is not corrected, the tutor offers a prompt or, finally, the right choice. It always finishes with positive social reinforcement from the tutor: an expression of support or a gesture of encouragement. This technique is simple, but we should make sure that the tutor gives enough time to the tutee so that the correct answer is found by him- or herself. In some sessions, the tutee's reading can be audio-recorded to check the quality of his or her technique.

In the next 15 minutes, the activities focus on text understanding. After thinking about whether the initial hypothesis has been fulfilled or not, the tutor helps the tutee to discover (often by the context information) unknown words, which he or she has previously pre-pared (using a dictionary, if necessary). The main ideas are designated and some different difficulty level activities are answered. Some of them require simply retrieving informa-tion that is literally in the text; others require some interpretation (inferring answers from the partial information that the text offers); and finally, the most interesting part is bring-ing into play the pair's reflection, since they have to infer or assess information that does not appear in the text.

Activity sheets try to include as rich a range as possible of reading comprehension activities: closed and open-ended questions; extracting main ideas or conclusions; high-lighting; sorting or classifying; and relating or making schemes. These always have the purpose of returning students to the hypothesis and the read text, through a reduced number of questions that can be resolved in the stipulated time. Where there is not enough time to finish the questions, it remains in the hands of the tutor or the teacher to expect them to be finished at home, or to reduce the activities while they are working.

When students work in a foreign language, pairs are provided with a language support that contains guidelines, located on the activity sheet as shown in the example (Figure 8.3); thus helping both students to keep the conversation in the learning language and avoid transferring to their first language.

The aim of the activity sheets is to serve as examples for the tutors in order to allow them—once they are familiar with formats, text characteristics and the variety of activities—to develop similar materials, under the teacher's supervision. The elaboration of teaching materials by students is, without doubt, a good learning opportunity. Therefore, tutors will be asked to develop at least two activity sheets. Teachers will determine the form of assistance for the creation of these materials. However, we suggest mainly indi-vidual work—since it will serve as an evaluation of the tutor—with varying degrees of support: from autonomous homework (that most of the tutors can make), to more assisted

LANGUAGE SUPPORT

A BARREL OF FUN

Before reading . . .

TUTOR	TUTEE
Do you think you are going to enjoy this text? Why?	Yes, I think so/No, I don't Because . . .
In your opinion, what type of text are you going to read: a story, a comic, a poem or neither?	I think, it's a . . . In my opinion, it's a . . .
Why do you think so?	Because...

Reading comprehension

Tutor	Tutee
1 Did you guess that the text is about different kinds of texts related to fun? How could you guess this?	Yes, I did / No, I didn't. Because I . . .
2 Decide if these sentences are True or False.	Sentences.............are true. Sentences.............are false.
3 Did you guess the solution to the riddles? Try to match each riddle with the right solution.	Yes, I did / No, I didn't. Riddle number 1 is . . .
4 Which of these riddles is the most difficult to understand for you? Why?	It's number . . . Because . . .
5 And, in your opinion, which is the funniest one? Why?	The funniest is . . . Because . . .
6 Try to explain the meaning, with your own words, of the idioms above.	The first idiom means that . . . The second idiom means that . . . The third idiom means that . . . The fourth idiom means that . . .
7 Choose one of the idioms related to your personal experience and explain the situation.	I choose the (1st, 2nd, 3rd, 4th) idiom. The situation was . . .

■ **Figure 8.3** Example of language support for the activity sheet

forms that can be done with other more expert tutors or the teacher's help. In any case, these sheets should always be checked by teachers before being used in the classroom.

One of these couple of sheets drawn up by each tutor may be photocopied and shared with the rest of the pairs in the class, and the other can be used only by the pair in particular. The first will offer us a rich 'sheet bank' to offer families. Activity sheets prepared by tutors increase the motivation of students and, above all, allow a greater adjustment to the characteristics or needs of each of the tutees.

In the case of family tutoring, we can opt for three ways for them to develop their own sheets: elaboration by family tutors; use of sheets made by student tutors in the school, but not used in class; or recommendations of books from children's literature, adjusted by age, which can be chosen by the tutee.

Returning to the session structure of *Reading in Pairs*, the last few minutes are engaged in expressive reading. In this case, after having achieved a thorough understanding of the text meaning, the tutee reads aloud the text for the last time. Full understanding will help tutees make a more expressive and natural reading by adjusting intonation, appropriating the text (and making changes that will improve understanding) and, finally, enriching the meaning of the text. It is a good time for tutors to help their tutees to realise progress and praise them for the effort they have made.

The session structure ends with the two blocks that are presented in parentheses in Figure 8.1, because they have no place in every session. One is the pair's self-assessment, which will occur in the last minutes, every four sessions or biweekly. And the other is the complementary activities, which will come into play only when pairs decide, or because they have time (in the case of the classroom), or they want to extend the session (in the case of in-family tutoring). We deal with these in the following sections.

The structure presented aims to guide the interaction between tutor and tutee to promote learning. But as we have mentioned, once the pair members know and internalise it (this can happen from the fourth or fifth session), it is necessary to offer the opportunity to develop a more flexible and creative use. In this sense, it is essential that pairs make decisions on the use of time: prioritising or reducing the time spent on each block. Thus, for example, where the tutee makes a quality mechanical reading, a pair can shorten the part of reading. Another pair, on the other hand, can devote more time and depth to comprehension activities or to complementary activities. In any case, adjustments must be reasoned in the self-assessment guideline and agreed with the teacher.

Even though we have made references to the teacher's role during peer tutoring sessions, it is worth remembering that this classroom organisation allows the development of actions that can be done within traditional classroom management but with more difficulty. Thus, during the sessions of peer tutoring, the teacher will offer immediate help to students (usually tutors) or pairs who request it; have the opportunity to hear as the students face their homework (enabling the teacher to get to know them better and to offer subsequently adjusted aid); observe and record difficulties and the pairs' progress (continuous assessment); and facilitate tutors in becoming aware of achievement in curricular learning.

Activity sheet development

One key element of the programme is the development of activity sheets which are offered by teachers for use in the class and at home, and which tutors prepare for their tutees. This is for two reasons. First, activity sheets guide the joint activity, but also provide the model for the tutors to develop their own. Second, when developing their activity sheets, tutors make one of their greatest efforts for learning, raising their own awareness that they are also learning from teaching their peers.

Three fundamental aspects are: type and origin of texts; typology of questions and activities; and validation and correction of sheets. The typology of texts must respond to the variety of textual discourse criteria. Teachers can select continuous texts (comics, poems, songs, recipes, letters, stories, news, menus, rules of games, riddles, listings, etc.); discontinuous texts (plans, schedules, tickets, graphics, posters, maps, advertisements, fact sheets, flyers, tables, etc.); or multiple texts, which combine continuous and discontinuous texts.

It is very important to choose texts that have units of meaning: beginning and ending, or having meaning by themselves. Texts should also be selected to respond to the interests and ages of students, with priority given to texts from their real lives. We suggest:

■ Asking students, in advance, to bring to class texts that they read at home and that interested them or that, despite interest in them, they have not understood completely.

■ Asking families that, during a weekend with their sons and daughters, they read a newspaper or a magazine and contribute with some text related to a topic of interest, whether it is news or opinion.

■ Asking teachers from other subjects, as history or science, to provide texts that are difficult to understand for students or that complement information from some class content.

It is also important to select texts of a difficulty slightly above the general level of the tutee's reading comprehension.

As we have seen in the previous section, the type of questions and reading comprehension activities should be varied. We suggest some strategies for the four objectives that should guide the activities of reading competence:

■ *Information retrieval*: think before reading what they know about the topic; predict content (guided by the theme, title, illustrations, context, experience, etc.); locate information at first glance (title, images, etc.); relate the topic with prior knowledge; anticipate potential problems (lexicon) and ways to resolve them.

■ *General understanding*: determine the main idea or topic; evaluate the importance of the information (essential, important, secondary ideas or indifferent); recognise sections, paragraphs and sentences.

■ *Interpretation and integration of ideas*: identify the text intent or purpose; compare and contrast information between different parts of the text; identify phrases that justify an idea, an opinion or rating.

■ *Meta-linguistic reflection*: critically consider the content of the text; take a position on the representation of displayed reality; assess the impact of some textual features.

The complementary activities section will suggest the creation of games, experimentation or discovery activities, such as memorising a poem, retelling a story to other students or finding more information about the text topic or the authors.

To end this section, it is important to note that validation and correction of activity sheets is crucial to guarantee their quality. Those prepared by teachers should respect the criteria and be shared with some other teachers to detect possible errors or enlarge some aspects if necessary. Those done/prepared by students should be corrected by teachers to also guarantee the desired quality.

Paired self-assessment

Students' awareness of their own learning and their partner's learning is essential to the success of *Reading in Pairs*. For this reason, self-assessment is a fundamental activity for programme development.

The pairs evaluate their progress biweekly. Aided by the paired self-assessment guidelines (Figure 8.4), both pair members agree on the need for improvement or on a satisfactory state, in different aspects relating to reading and reading comprehension. This self-assessment also considers the tutor's performance, in terms of explanations, reinforcement, modelling and control. In addition, in the comments section, students are asked to propose objectives for the next two weeks. These proposals range from reviewing complementary content, through improving relational aspects, to increasing attention.

These guidelines become more relevant when communicating the possibility of adjusting the time dedicated to the various periods of activity, by agreement between the pair and the teacher.

Also, if in the second half of the set of sessions, teachers opt to make changes to the pairs, records of the tutees' progress will be very helpful to the tutors who take responsibility for the learning of their new tutees.

In the first moments, probably by imitation of the teacher's role in the generalised model of education, tutors monopolise the responsibility for completing the guidelines. To avoid this, the teacher should remember and emphasise that self-assessment is the result of a dialogue and negotiation between both members of the pair, evaluating the progress of both, since the tutor's success depends on the tutee's progress and vice versa.

Complementary activities

This activity routine has the advantage of facilitating the establishment of good work dynamics, but has the disadvantage of repetition. In some pairs, allowing decisions about the time to devote to each activity block may be enough to break any feeling of monotony. In others, this may not be enough. Thus, it is convenient to generate a series of activities that break sporadically with those of the script.

Some of these activities, which we will call complementary, may be derived from the tasks contained in the activity sheets. Thus, for example, the preparation of oral presentations may be allowed at the start of the next class along with regular work. From any concerns which appear in the pair's self-assessment, tutors also prepare extra activities for the next session.

In the family context, complementary activities should provide the opportunity to extend the joint dialogue space. In this sense, the family tutor should never force them, but use them when it is worthwhile to extend a time which was pleasant but brief.

Criteria and activities for evaluation

The evaluation of the progress of students who participate in *Reading in Pairs* can be done by taking into account the information that comes from different sources. We suggest the following:

■ *Initial assessment.* At the beginning of the programme, all students undertake a language knowledge test to assess the actual level of their linguistic competence. The results can be useful in creating pairs. The test takes the same format as the activity sheets that students will work for in the programme, but in individual format.
■ *Follow-up of the paired self-assessment guideline.* Biweekly, the pair of students evaluates the academic progress of both components. The follow-up to their agreements offers valuable information on their progress.

Self-evaluation *Reading in Pairs*

Week from the _____ to the _____

Tutor _____ Tutee _____

Aims and proposals from last self-evaluation session (short comment about your improvements)

NI = need to improve, G = good

Before reading, we...	NI	G
Explore the characteristics of the text (title, pictures, photos, structure...)		
Make predictions about the contents of the text		
Talk about what we know from the topic		
Talk about possible difficulties		

During the tutor's reading	NI	G
The tutor reads correctly		
The tutee listens and follows the text		
The tutee appreciates the tutor's reading		

While reading together	NI	G
Tutor and tutee agree on how to read before starting		
Tutor and tutee read together and, at the same time, listen to each other		
Tutor listens to the tutee and waits for him or her		

PPP reading	NI	G
When reading, the tutee notices her or his mistakes		
When reading, the tutee notices mistakes and corrects them		
While the tutee is reading, the tutor stops the tutee if there is a mistake (PAUSE)		
While the tutee is reading and makes a mistake, the tutor stops him or her (PAUSE) and gives clues		
When the tutee corrects the mistake, the tutor encourages him or her to go on reading		

Reading comprehension	NI	G
We answer the questions together		
We share ideas and our previous knowledge to make good answers		
The tutee tries to answer the questions		
The tutor gives clues and helps the tutee with the answers		
At the end we talk about the main ideas of the text		

Tutee's reading	NI	G
The tutee reads the text showing understanding and good intonation The tutee improves his or her reading The tutee tries to read correctly The tutor appreciates the tutee's effort and how he or she improves his or her reading skills		
The tutor:	NI	G
Prepares the activity sheet Helps the tutee to read correctly Gives clues and ideas to help the tutee when he or she answers the questions Appreciates the tutee's effort		
The tutee:	NI	G
Tries to improve his or her reading skills and comprehension Participates and collaborates in understanding the text Appreciates the tutor's work		
Things we can improve for the next sessions		
Reading and comprehension:		
The tutor:		
The tutee:		

■ **Figure 8.4** Paired self-assessment guidelines

■ *Observations of pairs through record keeping.* The teacher observes the pair's performance helped by a grid (Figure 8.5), recording data referring to the tutor and the tutee, individually and as a pair. It is essential that teachers take the opportunity to track individuals or pairs, collecting aspects deemed most relevant—which is permitted by the management of the classroom in peer tutoring.

■ *Activity sheets made by tutors.* Once students have seen enough examples of activity sheets, they develop, as a minimum, two sheets for work in the classroom with their pair. This activity will serve for the final evaluation.

■ *Final test.* During the programme development, activities of some sessions can be used as continuous evaluation. Likewise, we can look at a sheet done at the end of the set of sessions to see the individual progress of each student in comparison with the results of the initial test.

TUTEE	He/she completes tasks						
	He/she is happy with the answers and aids						
	He/she makes questions and asks for help						
	He/she is comfortable, relaxed						
TUTOR	He/she prepares the topic, uses materials						
	His/her role reinforces self-esteem						
	He/she gives the tutee positive reinforcement						
	He/she gets actively involved in the tutee's learning						
PAIRS	They control time						
	They detect their own lack of knowledge						
	They acknowledge mistakes						
	They feel comfortable						
	They are interested in the task						
	They identify the meaning of new words						
	They activate previous knowledge						
	They don't look shy						
	Communication between them is fluid						
	They keep eye contact						
	Pairs of students	Tutor: Tutee:	Tutor: Tutee:	Tutor: Tutee:	Tutor: Tutee:	Tutor: Tutee:	Tutor: Tutee:

Further comments: Teacher's role, materials, organisation

■ **Figure 8.5** Teacher observation grid

■ *Portfolio assessment.* At the end of the tutorial sessions, students will have to submit a dossier containing the ordered activity sheets that have been worked on. Individually or in pairs, the tutor will provide additional material by way of explanations and short reflections on curricular improved aspects. At the same time, tutees should provide activities that they have completed at home.

■ *Information that comes from family tutoring.* For those students who also have used the programme at home with a family tutor, available information should be taken into account in global student progress.

TIMING

While schools can take different decisions about how the programme can achieve in the school calendar, we suggest by way of example:

■ *Initial assessment, previous training and pair-matching sessions.* It is advisable to devote two or three sessions to this essential phase for the functioning of the programme. Initial training is a real investment for the success of tutoring sessions.

■ *Activities in pairs with a common structure of activities for all.* Despite the variability depending on the characteristics of the student body, it is recommended to use four sessions in which all students have the same routine activities. The main function of the teacher, during this period, is to mark the change of activity, although, of course, not all pairs will have finished each section. Depending on the students' capabilities, teachers can transfer control time to the pairs sooner. In any case, it is convenient to inform students previously about this opportunity, in order that they can reflect how to manage it.

■ *Adjustment of activity structure by each pair.* During the following six sessions, each student pair will need to make decisions about the amount of time to be devoted to each block of activities. Every pair can reduce or extend the time of each block under two considerations; but they cannot unreasonably delete any block and cannot over-run time at the end of the session.

■ *Creation of activity sheets by tutors.* For at least the two final sessions, students work with activity sheets developed by the tutors themselves and supervised by teachers. Each tutor will be elaborating two sheets, one destined for the rest of the pairs and the other will be reserved for working on in his or her own pair. Logically, the rest of the sheets prepared by students should be passed out to families who require them.

■ *Final evaluation and closing activities.* Schools have to book at least two sessions for final evaluation of the programme. This can be done in many ways. The less formal way could be to ask students—individually, in pairs or in small groups—to think about the positive and negative elements of the experience. Combining the results, teachers will know the opinions of the group and be able to generate a helpful debate. Otherwise, a more formal but less spontaneous way is to use a survey or questionnaire.

Now the basis and characteristics of *Reading in Pairs* have been explained, the next chapter will present evidence about its impact on fluency, reading comprehension, reader self-concept and family involvement.

9

READING IN PAIRS

DOES IT WORK?

The *Reading in Pairs* programme is currently implemented through networks of centres in several areas of the Spanish state and Chile. Some studies have been developed, which focus mostly on assessing impact on fluency, reading comprehension, self-concept, family involvement and the network of centres. In all cases, the data collection procedure is characterised by mixed methods, combining a quasi-experimental approach (pretest/posttest) with a qualitative approach, based on data obtained from observation and interaction analyses of subsamples of pairs, student and family questionnaires, semistructured interviews with teachers and focus groups with samples of students, families and teachers. Below, we present some data from this research, which provides empirical evidence on the potential of the programme.

READING FLUENCY IMPROVEMENT

Valdebenito and Duran (2013) were interested in knowing the impact of *Reading in Pairs* on fluency in reading (understood as speed, accuracy, prosody, understanding and interpretation); their research obtained the quantitative results shown in Table 9.1.

Results showed significant differences between measurements at pretest and posttest, both in the intervention group (students who participated in *Reading in Pairs*) and in the control group. This is because all students participated in school activities favouring the practice of reading in the classroom. However, the effect size for these improvements was medium for the control group ($d = .60$) and large ($d = .82$) for the intervention group.

Both fixed-reciprocal tutoring and separate tutors and tutees achieved statistically significant differences with large effect sizes, which indicates that, regardless of the role assumed by the students, the programme was effective for improving reading fluency. The analysis of the interaction of pairs gives extensive evidence of related behaviours that affect the development of fluency. These behaviours take place in different types of reading aloud that come into play in the first part of the session: tutor reading, Reading Together, PPP reading and expressive reading. Throughout these readings, the tutor has the opportunity to read aloud with an audience, to actively listen and deliver monitoring. The tutee listens actively, receives modelling, reads aloud with an audience, receives monitoring and recites.

■ **Table 9.1** Results in reading fluency

Group	N	Mean pretest	Standard deviation	Mean posttest	Standard deviation	p
Intervention	127	57.64	19.35	73.87	20.41	.00
Control	120	46.53	19.51	58.14	19.00	.00
Fixed tutoring	105	60.45	19.58	78.44	18.73	.00
Reciprocal tutoring	22	46.32	9.82	52.05	12.59	.01
Tutor	54	68.42	18.09	83.40	17.04	.00
Tutee	51	52.00	17.58	73.20	19.15	.00

Students were consulted on improvements related to fluency and expressed the following: 'Thanks to the help of my partner, I have much improved in reading, respect punctuation marks and now I read faster' (Student 69, Centre 2); 'I've learned to pronounce better and read faster' (Student 105, Centre 3); and 'I have been taught to stand on the semicolons and to read better' (Student 126, Centre 4).

READING COMPREHENSION IMPROVEMENT

Because of the importance of comprehension in reading competence, the effects of *Reading in Pairs* on reading comprehension have been examined. The results from Flores and Duran's (2015) study are shown in Table 9.2, which also shows the scores in reading comprehension.

No statistically significant differences were observed between the control group and the intervention group in the pretest. It was thus confirmed that there were no initial differences between the two groups of the sample. In terms of the analysis within groups (pre- versus posttest), no statistically significant differences were observed in the control group, but there were statistically significant differences in the intervention group between the pre- and posttests. Findings also showed statistically significant improvements for both tutors and tutees and for the reciprocal-role model. These results indicate a general improvement in reading comprehension for students who took part in *Reading in Pairs*.

Through the analysis of the interaction of a subsample of pairs, we were able to confirm that the segments before and after reading contributed to creating a communicative exchange space which positively influenced reading comprehension development, with a high frequency recorded in text exploration, previous knowledge activation, generating hypotheses (prereading) and solving comprehension questions (postreading).

All these scaffolding processes may have fostered knowledge construction and may have aided in reading comprehension improvement. In the tutors' case, this fact could be explained by the use of complex strategies of selection, breaking down and reasoning. These strategies seek to help the tutees with text understanding, by giving them meaningful and close examples to try to promote their reflection and the elaboration of coherent answers, which are adjusted to the demands of text comprehension.

Likewise, all the teachers interviewed highlighted the progress of their students in general text understanding and the positive difference existing between levels of understanding at the beginning of the programme, and those achieved at the end. In addition, they

■ **Table 9.2** Results in reading comprehension

Group	N	Time	Mean (standard deviation)	p	Effect size
Comparison	136	Pre	53.15 (23.32)	.01	.16
		Post	56.88 (23.32)		
Intervention	441	Pre	49.87 (29.19)	< .01	.30
		Post	58.76 (29.19)		
Tutors	172	Pre	61.81 (22.69)	< .01	.36
		Post	69.97 (22.69)		
Tutees	173	Pre	42.20 (25.39)	< .01	.39
		Post	52.04 (25.39)		
Reciprocal tutoring	96	Pre	52.70 (22.73)	< .01	.37
		Post	61.17 (22.73)		

recognised the mediating role of tutors, in offering support and guides for tutee under-standing, while trying to avoid giving direct answers.

The perceptions of students also point to similar results. Students were considered to have improved their reading comprehension. The influence of peer tutoring stands out in their appraisals: 'You learn because you read it, ask questions and return to read' (Student 44, Centre 2); '. . . while you explain one thing, you recall it better' (Student 77, Centre 3); or '. . . because with your mates you feel more confident and they explain it better' (Student 142, Centre 4).

READING SELF-CONCEPT IMPROVEMENT

Self-concept as a reader, or one's assessment of oneself as a text reader, is linked to aca-demic self-concept and has an important impact on the willingness of the students to learn. It is necessary to develop a positive reading self-image in the students so that they see themselves as good readers and feel able to improve their competence. Flores and Duran (2013) explored the effect of the improvement in fluency and reading comprehension on reading self-concept, assuming a mutual influence between reading and self-concept.

The quantitative results, collected in Table 9.3, show no statistically significant differ-ences between pre- and posttest in the analysis within groups in the comparison group, but we did observe statistically significant differences between pre- and posttest in the intervention group. The statistically significant improvements shown by the interven-tion group indicate that participation in the Reading in Pairs programme offers learning opportunities which foster the development of the reading self-concept.

Further analysis of the intervention group results shows differences according to tutor-ing type. A statistically significant improvement between the pre- and posttests is observed in the tutors' group. Likewise, the differences observed in the tutees' group and the group under reciprocal tutoring are not statistically significant, despite the fact that both groups show small progress. Of course, small group size may contribute to this finding.

The fact that, in reciprocal tutoring, students have only half the time to develop each role, and that in one of these two roles the reading self-concept improvement is not

■ **Table 9.3** Results in reading self-concept

Group	N	Time	Mean (standard deviation)	p	Effect size
Comparison	136	Pre	66.70 (17.03)	.57	.03
		Post	67.28 (17.03)		
Intervention	441	Pre	67.04 (21.42)	< .01	.11
		Post	69.39 (21.42)		
Tutors	172	Pre	68.39 (16.92)	< .01	.20
		Post	71.72 (16.92)		
Tutees	173	Pre	63.47 (18.81)	.08	.09
		Post	65.22 (18.81)		
Reciprocal tutoring	96	Pre	71.61 (16.85)	.20	.10
		Post	73.31 (16.85)		

significant, could possibly suggest that reading progress in reciprocal tutoring self-concept is minimal and, thus, not significant from a statistical point of view.

The analysis of the interaction of a subsample of pairs shows that the main difference between tutors and tutees may be to do with the attribution that students have about their reading improvement (let us not forget that tutees also progress in fluency and comprehension). However, while tutors improve their self-concept, in the development of the role and the opportunities it provides for perceiving themselves as good readers, tutees attributed their increase in reading to the tutor's merits and contributions, rather than to their own efforts. It is perhaps necessary that the teacher should intervene to correct this trend.

FAMILY INVOLVEMENT

In *Reading in Pairs*, family involvement is a key component, whereby parents and others assume the role of tutors of reading to their sons or daughters, on a voluntary basis from home. For this reason, we are interested in knowing the impact of family engagement in developing reading comprehension (Blanch, Duran, Valdebenito & Flores, 2013).

In this study, with a sample of 303 students and 223 families, the percentage of family involvement reached 73.6, which included mostly mothers. Taking the pretest results in reading comprehension, we pay attention to two groups: the 25% of students with the better results and the 25% of students with the worst results. As Table 9.4 shows, all the students with better initial scores in reading comprehension received family support. Only less than half of students from the other group received family support. This highlights the need to find mechanisms to involve families who have less experience in stimulating reading at home.

In order to detect the effect of different factors (family involvement and tutor or tutee role) on student reading comprehension performance, a statistical analysis was carried out. According to the results in Table 9.5, significant differences were found in reading comprehension (p < 0.001).

With reference to involvement, significant differences were found (p < .001) in favour of family implication, compared to the students without family tutoring. Also, some

▪ **Table 9.4** Family involvement and children with very high or low reading comprehension achievement

Comprehension pretest results	Pupils		Family involvement	N	%
	N	% (total sample)			
High reading comprehension	37	12.21	YES	37	100
			NO	0	0
Low reading comprehension	41	13.53	YES	19	46.34
			NO	22	53.66

differences (p < .001) were found according to the time variable in the posttest results, compared to the pretest.

With reference to the pre- and posttest results, the factor which explained the improvement in reading comprehension is family involvement, not being a tutor or tutee. The results showed the positive effect of family involvement in improving reading comprehension competence.

The analyses of the interaction of a sample of pairs formed by family tutors and their sons or daughters shows that family tutors followed the instructions suggested by the programme. Moreover, family tutors also made adjustments that contributed to the improvement of their son or daughter. Thus, family tutors spent 10.28% of the time in prereading interventions; 3.16% in Reading Together; 29.27% in tutee reading; 3.32% in expressive reading; 47.31% in reading comprehension; and 3.32% in extra activity.

In reading comprehension activities, families shared a relaxed time and sometimes started conversations that went beyond the questions suggested in the activity. It was one of the parts of the session where there was more interaction and intervention between family tutors and tutees. In their interventions, as Table 9.6 shows, families followed the programme suggestions (reading or paraphrasing the questions and praising) and made adjustments (focusing tutee's attention or encouraging thinking).

Students' perceptions regarding family support showed satisfaction with the support received from their mothers, fathers or other family members. They appreciated the fact that it helped them to understand, to expand vocabulary, to read more quickly and

▪ **Table 9.5** Reading comprehension according to family involvement, role and time

Family involvement	Role	N	Pretest		Posttest	
			M	SD	M	SD
	Tutor	123	58.30	19.46	66.21	20.36
	Tutee	100	51.07	20.01	65.27	20.31
Yes	Total	223	55.06	19.99	65.79	20.30
	Tutor	31	41.91	16.96	48.01	21.26
	Tutee	49	41.07	21.49	50.34	23.63
No	Total	80	41.40	19.75	49.47	22.63

■ **Table 9.6** Family tutor's intervention during the reading comprehension activities

Family tutor's interventions	Frequencies	Percentage
Orientation	105	35.1%
Reads the question	56	53.4%
Focuses the tutee's attention	35	33.3%
Repeats part of the question	14	13.3%
Comprehension	20	6.7%
Paraphrases the question	12	60.0%
Repeats the question aloud	8	40.0%
Strategies to find the answer	80	26.8%
Encourages to think by asking more questions	32	40.0%
Says the answer or part of it	20	25.0%
Explains the answer	18	22.5%
Points at the answer in the text	10	12.5%
Praise	94	31.4%

to develop strategies to accomplish the task. They were also pleased to share a unique moment with family tutors. Participating families emphasised advances in reading and understanding of texts, in predisposition to reading, intonation, acquisition of new knowledge and autonomous searching for information.

The involved families showed their satisfaction with the programme, highlighting it as a time that allowed them to spend a pleasant moment, beyond the observation of positive outcomes in their children's learning, from which to create a communicative atmosphere with their sons or daughters.

TEACHERS' ASSESSMENTS

Teachers who participate in Reading in Pairs networks are organised into pairs of teachers for each centre, and receive training on the programme by the GRAI, both face-to-face and in a virtual classroom. Peer learning is promoted not only among students, but also between teachers (in the pairs at each centre) and among centres (through the designated meetings and visits between schools) (Duran & Utset, 2014).

Results obtained through interviews, questionnaires and analysis of the interactions in the virtual classroom show that the involved teachers see peer tutoring as a powerful methodological resource. It promotes attention to diversity, allowing educational benefits from the student differences that are present in the classroom. It includes advantageous elements, both for students and for themselves. In this sense, it is important to depart from previous practice where a more skilled student simply helped another, to advance to a more complex format. In this latter scenario, the student tutor also learns, perhaps even more than his or her own tutee—through the challenges proposed to him or her, such as in creating teaching materials for the tutee.

Teachers consider paired self-assessment activities as an enriching process for students. The exchange of points of view and assessment of the work taking place in these spaces develops metacognition and generates excellent situations for reading self-concept development. This responsibility is seen as part of the motivational enhancement of students.

Teachers point out that family participation in *Reading in Pairs* has a decisive influence on reading skills improvement. Still, they express concern about the difficulties of reaching the families who most need it and they highly value those that are involved, recognising progress in the learning achieved by students. They conclude that the involvement of the families of students who would receive more benefit requires patient and laborious work by the school, using those parents who have already participated in previous editions of *Reading in Pairs* in order to convey 'peer' satisfaction and motivation to participate.

In addition to all these data, the teachers who implement the programme in their local schools through the *Reading in Pairs* network apply a pre- and posttest reading comprehension test and a questionnaire for students and families. For them, the results of these instruments are good evidence to make decisions for keeping the programme or not, and for adjusting it to their context. Up to now, more than 95% of schools have decided to keep the programme, turning an innovation into a regular methodology in their schools.

PART III

ORGANISING AND IMPLEMENTING PEER TUTORING

10

PLANNING

CONTEXT, OBJECTIVES, MATERIALS, RECRUITMENT, SELECTION AND CONTACT

Peer tutoring complements the work teachers do in school, rather than replicating or replacing it. Freed from the necessity to 'hear children read' with the same degree of frequency, teachers can devote more time to planning and refining the more technical aspects of their professional work. If a school has only a few hours of teaching time to devote to helping children with reading, the evidence strongly suggests it will be much more cost-effective to use that time to train and support peers to tutor, rather than offer the children a fragmentary and irregular direct teaching service from a professional.

This chapter will provide information on how to set up and plan your peer tutoring in reading programme and is linked with a 'Planning Proforma' which is available on the eResources website. This is an action checklist on which to write your planning decisions as you make them. It is intended to ensure that you have thought of everything and that nothing can go wrong. You might want to look at it in the course of reading this chapter.

Do not assume that peer tutoring is a purely 'remedial' technique. Certainly, it has proven useful with children who have made a start with reading but do not seem to be progressing. Likewise, children labelled 'dyslexic' or all those who have difficulties in reading may benefit. But many schools have adopted the method for use across whole year groups and age ranges—for all children of all levels of ability. Everyone needs to develop reading competence, along all the school years.

So how do we set it up? A number of factors should be taken into consideration when planning the establishment of a peer tutoring project and when implementing it in daily practice. These factors will be discussed in the present and following chapters and are grouped under these headings: Context, Objectives, Materials, Recruitment, Selection and Matching, Organisation of Contact, Training, Support and Monitoring, Feedback and Evaluation.

CONTEXT

When starting to plan your peer tutoring programme, consider whether you will combine peer tutoring at school with a home component as well, involving students' parents (such as in the PR and *Reading in Pairs* programmes described in previous chapters). However, it is important that teachers do not see in peer tutoring a means of giving children extra reading practice, while they remain under the direct supervision and control of a professional, as an alternative to the possibly more challenging development of involving the children's parents in this exercise at home. Parents acting as reading helpers at home have great strengths, as well as weaknesses, in this role, which are different to those of either peer tutors or professional teachers.

The first and perhaps major question when planning a peer tutoring programme is: Who has the time, energy and commitment to set up the programme? In any school, a minimum of two enthusiastic teachers is preferable. A single teacher who tries to set up a scheme in isolation from the rest of the staff will find it a struggle, especially if the principal of the school is barely tolerant of the proposal. Two teachers working together can show students the meaning of pair working and cooperation in a practical way—and two heads are better than one!

Secondly, consideration should be given to the nature of the school's catchment area, the degree of reading difficulty common to the pupils, the existence of minority groups whose needs may be slightly different, and the existing relationships between school and community. From this will come an estimate of how much time and energy needs pouring into the project to ensure its success, or (to put it another way) how hard it is going to be.

Next, some thought about the organisational context of the school is required. What are reading standards in the school like generally? If they are alarmingly low, it may be unwise to launch a peer tutor project, if all it serves to do is conceal fundamental flaws in the organisation of teaching reading in school. Likewise, if there is division among the teaching staff, a peer tutor project could be used as a scapegoat for one of the factions, who might be happy to see the project fail. It is worth pondering whether there are any other social or political factors which may sabotage the project.

OBJECTIVES

It is important to be clear about your objectives, since if you are not clear what outcome(s) you are hoping for, you will not be able to tell whether the project was a success or not. However, life is full of surprises, so you may find some positive effects which you had not expected.

At this point, a suitable target group of children can be identified, in terms of ages, reading level, class membership and numbers involved. There is a lot to be said for building in some success for a school's first experience, so it would be unwise to start by targeting a large number of children with severe reading difficulties. Consideration of the overall number of pupils to be involved is necessary as well. An initial target group of a small number of children with a range of reading ability is probably the best bet. Resist any temptation to include 'just one more' or, before you know it, the whole thing will become unmanageable. Particularly for a first venture, it is important to be able to closely monitor a small number of children. Do not worry about those who have to be 'excluded'. They can have a turn later, or be incorporated into the project as your organisation becomes more fluent and automatic. Furthermore, if any evaluation is to be carried out, it will be useful to also check the progress of a comparison group of children who have not been involved in the peer tutoring.

Do not pick a few children from many different classes. It is best if the target group already has a good deal of social contact in the school. If you can involve a substantial number in the project, the children will begin to encourage and reinforce each other.

Deliberately try to create a group social ethos which is positive towards the project. If children feel isolated by being labelled as peer tutors or tutees (although this is unusual), they might feel picked on and stigmatised by the adults who selected them. Including a wider range of reading abilities in the project helps to avoid any playground mythology that peer tutoring is for the backward. In this context, you will also need to think about how the project might relate to the school's existing programmes for teaching reading.

So what sort of gains might be expected to accrue from the project? Are you hoping just for improvements in reading? Accuracy? Comprehension? Fluency? Are you also looking for improved attitudes towards reading? Or improved attitudes to the self—better confidence, self-esteem, and so on? Are you looking to extend the children's experience of reading—to different materials, different places or at higher levels of difficulty? Or are you using the project for other purposes, such as to improve peer relationships generally, give the school a better image locally or increase the enrolment rate?

When defining the programme goals, recall that peer tutor projects often include social gains among their objectives. Thus in a cross-age project, one aim may be to increase a sense of cohesiveness and caring between older and younger children. In a project which matches children across genders and races, familiarisation may also yield social benefits.

Remember too that peer tutoring should be characterised by explication of objectives for the tutors. Well-organised peer tutoring should involve 'learning by teaching' for the tutors, who should also gain socially and in terms of reading skill, attitudes and self-esteem. If you cannot specify valid educational objectives for the tutors, you are not using true peer tutoring and students can feel that they are merely being 'used'—and their parents will rightly object to this.

Whatever goals you pursue, you do need to be honest about your objectives. Of course, you may find that different teachers who are involved actually have different objectives for the project. Subsequently, one could consider the project a success while the other considers it a failure. Without honesty about objectives, you can get into a terrible tangle.

MATERIALS

Remember that restricting the readability of the material used to the tutee's current independent readability level fails to challenge the tutee and runs the risk of boring the tutor. However, the readability of the material should certainly have a ceiling placed upon it at the tutor's independent reading level. We must avoid at all costs the tutee presenting the tutor with failure, or the generation of confusion through both tutee and tutor losing touch with the text.

Where there is a large reading ability difference between tutors and tutees, the readability of the material might need controlling to a point somewhat below the tutor's level, but still above that of the tutee. However, avoid big ability differentials wherever possible. The tutor will certainly gain more and remain more interested if the reading ability differential is only two or three years.

While some books in school might already be graded for readability—and pairs can thereby easily ensure that tutors are not challenged—it can become problematic once the pairs begin to explore more widely the issue of readability of materials. Therefore, pairs should be taught a simple way of checking the readability of books. It should be made perfectly clear to them why they need to know and implement this. As children become more used to each other and to choosing texts, they will develop their own more sophisticated methods, about which you can hold a class discussion.

When given free choice, many children develop or learn the skills of choosing appropriately within two or three weeks, and teachers should avoid interfering during the early period of a project in this respect. However, a small minority of children may still be all at sea about choosing appropriate books, even after this time. At this juncture, teachers may need to step in to give a little gentle assistance and guidance—the aim being to develop choosing skills in the child, rather than merely doing it for the child.

Some children will wish to bring in books or magazines from home, and this should certainly be encouraged up to a point, provided the readability level remains within the tutor's competence. Some children may begin bringing in comics, which may also be accepted up to a point; but if it gets out of hand, be prepared to impose a quota or ration on comic content, and enrich their reading diet with other kinds of texts which are acceptable.

If you are following the 'rules' to the letter, you will give children completely free choice of reading materials. However, with very young or very slow readers, or those whose parents are of limited literacy, you might want to set a readability ceiling below which the children have free choice.

As with parent tutoring, the sources for reading materials can be many and various. In view of the increased amount of practice and increased speed of reading which is associated with peer tutoring techniques, the availability of reading material must be scrutinised. The number of books that the children get through will amaze you. Ideally, they should be able to change their books on every occasion they are in contact. This raises questions about the existing quantity, quality, variety and means of access. The children's demand for reading material interesting to them might double or treble. The demand for nonfiction material is especially likely to increase. Logistically, it may be easier to mount a special additional collection in some convenient and accessible area. All kinds of reading materials, including e-books, should be displayed in an accessible and stimulating way.

If the school has an existing system for lending books, this may need extending to all books in the school, including supplementary readers, other fiction and nonfiction books in classrooms and in the school library, and so on. If you use basal readers (a 'reading scheme' in the UK), you will need to make a judgement about whether those books should be included or not (most schools decide not; and in any event, the children would not choose them). The local libraries service may be helpful in providing a special loan collection of attractive books just for use by the project children. Alternatively, you might be able to siphon off a 'special collection' for the project children from sources within school.

The existing system for recording loans of books should be scrutinised. A peer tutor project will usually greatly increase loan rates and put heavy strain on the current recording system, especially if it is rather unwieldy or elaborate. You might wish to streamline the system, devolve some of the work and responsibility on to the children, or arrange for volunteer parents to operate the loan arrangements.

Information about access to local libraries should be gathered and made available. You may wish to incorporate a visit to the local public library as part of your project. Visiting the public library, and allowing pairs to wander around and explore and select books together, is a pleasurable and valuable activity in relation to book and literacy promotion. Furthermore, you may be able to organise other literacy related activities during the project. The children will soon start recommending books to each other and you may want to give them a noticeboard, to enable reading circles to flourish and to use other ways of communicating their views—but don't make it too much like hard work for the children!

When your peer tutoring programme does not work with books, but with short texts, try to select them in relation to similar readability guides, with a variety of types or genres and with a coherent and complete meaning within the text. It could be very useful to work with texts that the students will need to use in their schoolwork, or with texts provided by students which they want to understand, but with which they have expressed difficulties.

Some peer tutoring programmes, like *Reading in Pairs*, suggest that tutors who have become familiar with materials or activity sheets should have the opportunity to select texts and create learning activities for their tutees. Creating pedagogical material could be a good way to enhance the tutor's learning.

RECRUITMENT

Assuming that a group meeting in school for tutors and tutees is to be a feature of the project at some stage, communication must be established with the target children prior to any request to attend a meeting. Preparatory information can be communicated verbally and in writing.

Also, the question of parental agreement often arises in connection with peer tutor projects. Experience shows that involvement in such a project is usually sufficiently interesting for the children to result in many of them mentioning it at home. This can lead to some parents getting very strange ideas about what is going on. Parents will want some idea as to why their children have been chosen, especially if their child is to be a tutor, or if they think their tutee child is considered to have a reading difficulty which has never been made clear to the parents before.

If you have chosen some target children at random for 'experimental' purposes, you will need to tell their parents of this. It is thus usually desirable for a brief note from school to be taken home by both tutors and tutees, explaining the project very simply. The eResources website includes a specimen leaflet for parents about peer tutoring. This should reassure parents that the project will have both academic and social benefits for tutors as well as tutees. Of course, an excellent way to explain to parents what peer tutoring is could be inviting them to take part in the project. Receiving training and playing the role of reading tutor at home is a good way to deeply understand tutoring, including peer tutoring.

You may wish to raise your public profile by using posters or the local media. It is often effective to whip up enthusiasm in the children at school. There may be some value in having children write out their own letters of invitation to their tutee or tutor, or in developing the format of the letter as a group project. This generates social cohesion right from the onset of the project.

If there are children you see as being in particular need of involvement in your project, you may wish to make special efforts beforehand. However, as has been said before, do not worry if not all the 'most needy' cases in the neighbourhood do not get involved in your first project. It is very important that your first is successful. Once you achieve that, the good news will ripple around the community, and you will find that subsequent recruitment becomes easier and easier as momentum gathers.

SELECTION AND MATCHING OF CHILDREN

All teachers have experienced the great variations in general maturity levels shown by classes in succeeding years. It would be particularly unwise to mount a project involving many children whose maturity to cope with the procedure is in grave doubt. In cases of uncertainty, it is usually wisest to start a small pilot project with a few of the most mature children in the class acting as tutors, to enable further tutors to be added to the project subsequently as a 'privilege'.

Where the children have already been used to taking on a degree of responsibility for their own learning and/or working on cooperative projects in small groups, they may be expected to take to peer tutoring more readily.

In some cases, the gender balance in the class can represent a problem, particularly if there are more girls than boys, since some boys might express extreme reluctance at the prospect of being tutored by a girl. Needless to say, this reluctance often disappears fairly quickly in class where the teacher allocates a female tutor to a male tutee and instructs them to get on with it; but the tutee may still have difficulty justifying what is going on to his friends in the playground.

The chronological ages of the tutors and tutees need considering separately. Do not assume that age and ability are synonymous. If you intend to use tutors who are consider-ably older than the tutees, unless you are fortunate enough to teach a vertically grouped class, you are likely to find the organisation of the project considerably more complicated. This is especially true if the tutors are to be imported from another school. Same-age tutoring within one class is by far the easiest to organise. And, of course, in every class there is enough diversity to enable students to learn from each other.

The reading ability of the children is the critical factor in selection and matching of tutors and tutees. As we have said, as a general rule it is probably as well to keep a dif-ferential of about two years' reading age between tutors and tutees. Where same-age tutoring is to be established with a whole class, the children can be ranked in terms of scores on reading tests, and a line drawn through the middle of the ranked list to separate tutors at the top from tutees at the bottom. Then the most able tutor is paired with the most able tutee, and so on. Other criteria for ranking could include basal reader/reading scheme level, the teacher's observations or intuitive judgement.

It is possible to use reciprocal peer tutoring, particularly in peer tutoring projects where pairs work with activity sheets that tutors can prepare before the session. In this case, stu-dents are matched in pairs with a similar reading ability, and the tutor role is exchanged every alternate session. This arrangement enables tutors to 'gain' the required difference in reading ability by preparing the materials in advance.

However, the children's reading ability is not the only factor which must be taken into account. Pre-existing social relationships in the peer group must also be considered. To pair children with their 'best friends' of the moment might not be a good idea, particularly as the friendship may be of short duration. Obviously, it would be undesirable to pair a child with another child with whom there is a pre-existing poor relationship. Another of the advantages of a same-age project is that one teacher is much more likely to know all the children involved, and thus can be more sensitive in taking social relationships into account.

It may or may not be desirable to take the individual preferences of the children themselves into account in some way. Some children may surprise you with the matu-rity they show in selecting a tutor they think would be effective in this role. However, to allow completely free child selection of tutors is likely to result in chaos. Quite apart from the question of maintaining the requisite differential in reading ability, some tutors would be over-chosen—others not chosen at all.

When students are organised in pairs, it could be that some of them say they do not want to work together. See if they can suggest some changes in the pairs. However, a change is not always a good solution. A problem in one pair could become a problem in many pairs. It is better to make it understood that peer tutoring is a way to learn to cooperate with others, especially with those who are not your current best friends. And, of course, give students tools to improve their relationships. One of these could be that all students individually think about the best characteristics of a good teacher, or tutor and of a good student or tutee. Then as a first pair activity, they should seek to negotiate and agree a set of characteristics that they will try to follow. In the eResources website, there is an example of a guide to help with this.

One of the organisational difficulties with peer tutoring is the impact of absence from school of a tutor or tutee, because it is an active methodology. This impact and the degree of usual peer commitment help explain why peer tutoring can have effects in improving attendance. It is always worthwhile to nominate a spare, stand-by or supply tutor or two, to ensure that absence from school of the usual tutor can be covered. Children acting as spare tutors need to be particularly stable, sociable and competent at reading, since they will have to work with a wide range of tutees. However, do not worry about imposing a burden on the spare tutors, as they may be expected to benefit the most in terms of increases in reading ability and self-esteem. The other obvious strategy for coping with absence is to attempt to rematch those children without partners, perhaps involving a change of role for some.

ORGANISATION OF CONTACT

A basic decision is whether the tutoring is to occur wholly in class time, wholly in the children's break or recess time, or in a combination of both.

If the tutoring is to occur wholly in class time, it can be kept under teacher supervision. However, it will usually require scheduling. If the tutoring is to occur in the children's break time, more mature pairs can be left to make their own arrangements satisfactorily. This arrangement is a much greater imposition on tutors and tutees alike, however; and the momentum of the project may begin to peter out as the novelty begins to wear off. Some scheduling may thus be necessary, even during the children's recess time, so that the size and nature of the commitment involved is visible to all from the outset. The best compromise is usually to schedule some minimum contact for class time (perhaps three sessions per week), but allow the opportunity for pairs to do additional tutoring in their own break time if they so wish.

Finding the physical space to accommodate the pairs can be a challenge. Because peer tutoring is based on the help every student gives each other, teachers gather a great number of pairs in the same place. In peer tutoring sessions students have to read aloud, talk to each other . . . and be noisy. A good tip is to keep pairs as close as possible. If their heads are close to each other, they should not have to raise their voices and disturb other pairs. Pairs should sit down close together and side-by-side, to share the reading materials. It could be convenient to have access to supports such as dictionaries or online documents.

So, in a cross-age tutor project within a school, particularly where two full classes are involved, it is possible for half the pairs to work in the tutee's classroom and the other half in the tutor's classroom. But even then, providing an additional room is advisable. In this respect, it is quieter in the different rooms and pairs do not disturb one another. Finding physical space for the tutoring to occur during recess times may be considerably more difficult if there are problems of recess time supervision and/or if children are not allowed access to classrooms.

Each individual tutoring period should last for a minimum of 15 minutes. Little that is worthwhile can occur in less time than this, after you have allowed for lack of punctuality and general settling down. If it is possible for the really enthusiastic to continue for over 20 minutes, this is advantageous. It might be possible for the minimum 15 minutes to occur just before a natural break time, but do provide for the possibility of children continuing into their own break time if they so desire.

The frequency of tutorial contact should be three times each week, as a basic minimum, to ensure that the project has a significant and measurable impact. If peer tutoring occurs less frequently, it may have benefits, but they may not be measurable. If four or five contacts per week can be arranged, so much the better. Children involved in peer tutor projects rarely object to daily tutoring, as most of them find it interesting and rewarding. Some pairs may organise their own impromptu sessions in their own break times, whether the teacher likes it or not.

Keep in mind that timing of the tutoring periods and scheduling the number of tutorial contacts throughout the week should be tuned to the objectives of your programme. When aiming for complex skills, such as practising the use of various reading strategies for optimising reading comprehension (e.g. as is the case in the *One Book for Two* project described in more detail previously), you would be better to include a longer session instead of two or three short sessions. This will allow children to get deeply involved in a text in order to practise the different reading strategies in combination, and to get as close as possible to authentic reading and the use of strategies in a relevant way.

The project should be launched with reference to an initial fixed period of commitment. It is useful for both tutors and tutees to be clear about what they are letting themselves in for, and how long a course they need to be able to sustain. A minimum project period of six weeks is suggested, since it will barely be possible to discern significant impact in less time than this. Popular project periods are eight weeks and ten weeks, which fit comfortably within an average term or semester. Shorter 'trial' periods are probably better with younger or less motivated children. Fit this neatly into a term or semester, so the active period is not broken by a long holiday or vacation. You might also need to avoid other major conflicting or disruptive events.

It is not desirable to fix a period of longer than 12 weeks for an initial commitment. It will be much better to review the project at the end of a short initial period, to evaluate the outcomes and make decisions about future directions jointly with the children, rather than letting the whole thing drift on interminably until it runs out of steam.

Let us pause now and digest what we have learned so far. Then when we are ready, we can proceed to the next chapter, which covers training, monitoring, feedback and evaluation.

OPERATING

TRAINING, MONITORING, FEEDBACK AND EVALUATION

TRAINING OF SCHOOL STAFF

First, ensure that the project coordinators actually know what they are talking about. They need to have not only read about peer tutoring but actually to have tried the techniques—preferably with a few different children. You can't talk sensibly to children about it until you have done it yourself.

A live demonstration (or failing that, a demonstration on video) is highly desirable. Contact with other local schools already using the technique, or with the local teacher resource centre, school psychological service or other advisory service, may provide such an opportunity. Following this, practice is necessary. The project organisers should seize any opportunity to practise the technique on a range of children—preferably not the intended target children.

It is always helpful if other school staff are briefed about the method and the project. The more the project is shared by other teachers and seen as a school project, the more possibilities develop for peer tutoring to become a regular and sustainable practice in the school. You may therefore wish to run a brief in-service training session for your colleagues, to ensure that some minimal level of consistent awareness exists among them before proceeding further. Try to ensure there is an opportunity for doubts and reservations to be tabled and discussed. To help you with this, reproducible presentations about methods and research background can be found on the eResources website.

TRAINING OF TUTORS AND TUTEES

In setting the date for your 'launch' training meeting with tutors and tutees, you need to establish the length of the initial period of the project—six, eight or ten weeks. This initial commitment creates clear expectations for tutees and tutors. It also ensures that the majority use the technique frequently enough to become both fluent and practised in it, and also to see a significant change in the reading ability of the tutee, which should reinforce the tutors in continuing their use of the technique in the longer term.

It is neither effective nor ethically justifiable to turn the tutors loose on the unsuspecting tutees without giving them some form of training. Sometimes, the tutors and tutees are trained in two separate groups, but it is best to train them together. Have both at training meetings, so both receive exactly the same message and can practise straight away (although you can have a prior meeting just with the tutors as well, if you wish). The structure of the training for the tutors and tutees must be carefully delineated. The most suitable times and days for training must be established. One meeting may suffice, or perhaps two could be considered, in order to teach the phases of the method separately. When implementing more complex procedures in the peer tutoring sessions, or when you are aiming to practise some communication skills first as well, more training sessions might be needed.

You will need to identify one major meeting room and some additional, more private, practice spaces. Purely for the training meeting, it is very important that the tutees have already chosen books with which to practise, otherwise there will be a delay and melee while they rush about choosing. Their class teacher should have had them choose two books prior to the meeting for practice purposes. Left to their own devices, many will choose books which are too easy, so check that they have at least one book which is above their independent readability level.

Some 'lecturing' about the method and its effectiveness is inevitable, especially about the idea that tutors will learn by teaching their tutees—but keep it brief, and avoid long words and jargon. Also, avoid appearing patronising. A video or live role play between teachers on 'how *not* to do it' may be useful to break the ice, while making some very pertinent points. Written instructions about the method, perhaps accompanied by checklists or summary guidelines for ready reference, will be necessary. Readability of these should be kept low. The standard of production should be good to demonstrate that the project is important and professionally run. Do not give out written materials before talking—they should merely serve as a reminder of what everyone has learned.

A demonstration of how to do the peer tutoring is essential, either on video, or by role play between adults, or by a live demonstration with a cooperative and socially robust child tutored by a teacher. At subsequent meetings, tutors and tutees who have already experienced success with the technique will be available to give demonstrations (and/or offer testimonials). In this respect, you add interim continuous support to the prior training of students, a point we will discuss more in detail in the following section.

The advantages of the video are that it is easily seen and heard by a large group, which real live children may not be. Very brief clips of Reading Together and reading alone can be inserted at relevant points in your presentation. Choose two- to three-minute clips relevant to your audience. Never show a whole video programme—you will bore people. Make sure the equipment is working adequately for use with a large group and that you have your selected clips cued up, with any counter readings synchronised to the specific machine you are using. The video has the advantage of being predictable—more predictable than child actors! Perhaps most importantly, the unknown actors can also be criticised, so you can pause and make teaching points about what has and has not happened in the sequence shown. Information about where to obtain videos for training can be found on the eResources website.

You may wish to try making your own video. There are great advantages in having a video demonstration by local children with local accents. It helps to foster a sense of belonging and ownership. Bear in mind how the video is to be used, as detailed above. Do not try to compete with network television—you can't! Do not try to make a stand-alone self-explanatory programme. It won't work and will bore people. Talking things through and engaging in an interactive discussion with the children is necessary to point out the important aspects in the training.

Remember to include participants of different ages, reading levels, gender and ethnic origin, so you can choose the most appropriate for any particular audience and intersperse their actions with talk. However, do not underestimate the difficulty of achieving this.

Pay careful attention to obtaining good audio quality and remember, people rarely do for the camera what they did in rehearsal. There is also the problem that if your actors do the technique badly, you will not be able to 'criticise' the poor aspects for teaching purposes in front of their friends at subsequent showings. Video role play by teachers showing 'how not to do it' is invaluable for this.

At this stage of the training meeting, it is essential to encourage all children to actually practise the method. Express this as a standard expectation and tell the children in advance that it will be happening. The teachers or other professionals can then circulate and offer praise and/or further guidance as necessary. This monitoring of practice does require a high staffing ratio—one professional is unlikely to be able to cover more than five pairs during a brief practice period.

Pairs who are doing well can be praised and left to continue. Pairs who are struggling may need one of three levels of further coaching. First, give further verbal advice. If that doesn't work, try joining in with Reading Together to model the pacing and intonation through triad reading. Third, if all else fails, take the book or short text and demonstrate with the child yourself, then pass the book or short text back and let the pair continue with level one and two support.

Lastly, it is helpful to gather everyone back together and deal briefly with any other points of organisation—where the children can obtain books, how often, how the monitoring system will work, what to do if there are problems, and so on. After the practice is the time for any questions from the whole group.

At the end of the training meeting, children could be asked for a verbal or written decision on whether they wish to be included in the project, and possibly also be asked to indicate preferences for alternative forms of follow-up support. The whole meeting should generate a lively, exciting aura, so everyone feels they are part of a new experimental venture. Some projects hand out badges at launch meetings to foster a sense of belonging—and to turn children into walking advertisements for subsequent projects.

If the project involves parents or volunteers as tutors, the training session with them can follow the same structure in a more adapted and abbreviated way.

SUPPORT AND MONITORING

During the course of the project, it is important that the coordinating teacher keeps a close eye on how things are going, in order to nip any incipient problems in the bud. In the spirit of cooperation which permeates peer tutoring, the children themselves may be the first to report difficulty or seek help—and they should be stimulated to do so. Such self-referral may revolve around asking the meaning of words which are unfamiliar to both tutor and tutee. Children also should be encouraged to readily report difficulties in accommodating each other's habits without feeling that they are 'telling tales'.

Where a supervising teacher is present during the tutoring, much can be gleaned by observing individual pairs in rotation. The peer tutoring session is not an opportunity for the teacher to 'get on with some marking'. On the contrary, the teacher should either be setting a good example by reading silently or with a tutee, or should be circulating round the group, observing and guiding children as necessary. It is possible to ask a particularly expert child tutor (perhaps a stand-by tutor) who is not otherwise engaged to act as an observer in a similar way and report back to the teacher. The PR technique checklist previously mentioned (on the eResources website) will be useful for either teacher or peer monitor to help structure the observations. This checklist can also be used as a self-assessment device by more mature pairs. You might wish to use and discuss the checklists (on the eResources website), or your own observation criteria or priority points of attention you want to focus on, as you circulate to see how the pairs are doing.

In addition, it is often worthwhile calling occasional review meetings with tutors and tutees separately or together, in order to discuss in large or small groups how the project is going and what improvements could be made.

A most useful minimal form of monitoring is a diary or recording system. Children make a note of what and how much is read each session. At least each week, the supervising teacher should check the diaries and add further comments and praise, which serve to encourage both children. The teacher can add an official signature if required. A reproducible form suitable for this purpose can be found on the eResources website.

Some form of self-recording each session during the project is probably desirable. It is a tangible demonstration of achievement for the children and of considerable interest for the monitoring teacher. It is entirely logical that these records should be kept by the children themselves. Simple diaries can be kept by each pair (see the diary on the eResources website). The diary record asks the tutor and tutee to record what has been read, for how long (so they can be praised for doing more than the minimum, or restrained if they are doing too much), and with whom (so we can see how many different tutors have read with them and estimate the risk of inconsistent procedure). There is also space for the tutor to write some (hopefully positive) comment about the tutee's performance.

Even quite young children acting as tutors can prove to be surprisingly good at writing positive comments about their tutees. Learning to give and receive praise without embarrassment is a valuable component of peer tutor projects. Some tutors, however, soon run out of good things to say. To help those with a restricted vocabulary of praise, the Dictionary of Praise was devised. This can be found on the eResources website, and may be reproduced.

The record form offers a means to sustain monitoring of the project. Children could take the form home to show their parents. It also, of course, serves as a three-way accountability measure. While the teacher will see if the children aren't doing their bit, the children will see if the teacher hasn't bothered to sign the card or model good quality written praise. It can also serve as an emergency signalling system—if things aren't working out, a cry for help can be written on the card.

The easiest method for using diary cards is probably to have them colour coded by weeks, so it is very easy to see if one goes astray. When the week's card has been seen by the teacher, a new colour card for the ensuing week can be issued, which can be stapled on to the old one. The cards thus form an accumulating record of achievement. However, do not underestimate the teacher time involved in checking the cards weekly. If you have 15 pairs in your class and you spend 5 minutes each per week discussing their diary cards, that amounts to an hour and a quarter per week!

Naturally, there will be some children for whom this relatively lightweight form of monitoring will not suffice. You may wish to schedule individual meetings between teachers, tutors and tutees in school to resolve any difficulties which arise, or larger group 'booster' meetings for further practice and mutual feedback.

Some form of follow-up support and monitoring for the coordinating teacher(s) is also highly desirable, especially where the project is a first attempt, or the project leader is professionally isolated. Support may come from mentors within school or, perhaps even better, from some external consultant. Teachers should proactively recruit support of this kind.

FEEDBACK

Peer tutoring in children's reading is a collaborative venture between the three main participants—teachers, tutors and tutees. If the initiative is to become self-sustaining and to grow, all three parties need to feel valued and appreciated, consulted and empowered.

It is therefore important that after the stipulated initial 'trial' or experimental period, tutors and tutees share their views on the success or otherwise of the venture. At this point, they also need to make their own decision about where they are going to go from here. Some may choose to continue several days a week; some may wish to go on doing it, but less frequently; some may wish to try another kind of approach to reading; some may wish to try peer tutoring in another curriculum area such as spelling; while a few might wish to stop altogether.

Feedback meetings may include tutors and tutees all together or separately. More mature children may cope well with the former (remember peer tutoring makes them more confident), but younger children should perhaps have a separate meeting at which their views are gathered by a professional. Tutors and tutees can then meet up to hear the professionals' summary of both sets of views. You may expect to hear many contradictory opinions expressed at such meetings. Remember that it is important that they have a chance to give their views—that in itself has valuable effects. You may end up feeling that you cannot possibly follow all the contradictory advice given about making 'improvements', however!

A very simple way of presenting the favourable results and information to the children themselves is necessary to encourage them and promote further growth of confidence. A more 'scientific' collation will be necessary to present to interested colleagues. The information for this latter exercise need not necessarily be any less simple, merely different in emphasis.

At the end of the initial phase of the project, in the light of the evaluation and monitoring information, joint decisions have to be made about the future. At this point, the views of the children must be taken very much into account. Some may want to continue peer tutoring with the same frequency; others may wish to continue, but with a lesser frequency; while a few may want a complete rest, at least for a while.

When in doubt, a good rule of thumb is to go for the parsimonious option. It will be better to leave some of the children a little 'hungry', and have them pestering you to launch another project in six weeks' time, rather than let peer tutoring meander on indefinitely until it quietly expires. At this point of decision-making, also beware of trying to cater for a wide variety of choices from different tutoring pairs. The organisation of the project could become unbelievably complicated if you attempted to accommodate the varying desires for continuation of large numbers of children. It is probably as well to stick with what the majority votes for. Peer tutoring can thus be seen to be not only cooperative, but democratic as well.

The feedback meeting can be much more relaxed and informal than the training meeting. The professionals should give their feedback first, modelling the appropriate behaviour. Urge those who are usually quiet in meetings to offer a comment, however brief. If you have evaluation results for your project at this time, you could report those in summary. Do not give data about individual children. Specific numbers are probably best avoided except in private discussion with the pair themselves, and maybe not even then if the individual's scores are potentially misleading.

You will want to celebrate the success of the children, teachers and school. Schools have their own styles on these matters. Some form of certificate is often well-received, or perhaps an even grander badge. A reproducible certificate for this purpose can be found on the eResources website.

If you wish to discuss possible modifications to the technique for those pairs who feel ready to move on, there are other reproducible handouts, also on the eResources website.

EVALUATION

There is considerable virtue in building in some form of evaluation for the initial 'experimental' period of the project. This is especially true where the project is a first for the school. There may have been positive evaluation results from many other projects around the world, but that doesn't necessarily mean you made it work right there where you are. The evaluation of projects is considered in detail in Chapter 13.

Naturally, the first time that a school runs a project is the most difficult and consumes the most energy. Remember that teachers and students need to learn their new respective roles in peer tutoring. This needs time, support and focus—not only on what does not work well, but also on things that are working reasonably well. Once the teachers involved are familiar with the procedure, and all the required materials are to hand, the project can be run for subsequent target groups with much less hard work involved.

THE ROLE OF THE TEACHER IN PEER TUTORING

> Now that my students have already received initial training, they exactly know what to do and what not to do. And look, in these first sessions they are already working. What do I do?

This is an authentic comment made by a teacher in the first systematic application of one of the peer tutoring methods described in the preceding chapters. Certainly, peer tutoring radically modifies the role of the teacher in the classroom. Let's see, then, how the classroom becomes a richer and more democratic space; how the teacher's role acquires a transformative nature; and how management enables educational performance that could hardly be achieved in the traditional classroom.

Peer tutoring alters the organisation of the classroom, modifying the role of the teacher and his or her performance—it transforms the stage. Let us focus first on the main changes in the class.

A source of multiple learning opportunities and resources

> In my regular classes, the classroom is organised as a simultaneous chess game, in which the master, me, at the same time plays with twenty-something players, who are my students. Each student, each chessboard, has its needs . . . but I don't have time for all, and I have to move the pieces quickly, in an unadjusted way, without being able to comment on them . . . And, of course, I lose on many boards. On the other hand, in the peer tutoring sessions, the classroom becomes a chess tournament, where each pair makes his match, and I can see how they play, offer aid, comments . . . and I don't lose on any board!

This quotation is from the same teacher as the one above. It suggests that peer tutoring multiplies the sources of learning in the classroom, overcoming the 'radial' organisation where students only learn from the teacher, who offers them a little adjustable support to meet their personal needs. Peer tutoring moves to a richer form of organisation, where students not only learn from their teacher but also from their peers. This makes teachers feel that they 'don't lose on any board' and frees the teacher of the sense of frustration for not being able to reach everyone adequately.

Sharing the ability to teach

Teachers who use peer tutoring in their classes meet the challenge of sharing with their students—and perhaps their families—a competence, namely the ability to teach. If support is offered, students can teach—and learn by teaching—their peers. This has an impact on the students; they feel trusted and involved in developing the most valued activity in the schools. It also has an impact on the classroom organisation, developing a true learning community where *everyone* learns.

A microcosm of a more democratic society

The opportunity to take part in peer tutoring sessions allows teachers and students to experience that another kind of education is possible, based on the recognition and appreciation of all, the positive use of differences between students and the promotion of mutual aid. And what is more important, this microcosm is also a proof that another more democratic and participatory society is possible too.

Noise, but learning

In peer tutoring sessions, students interact with each other, often vividly and passionately. Sometimes, we promote that both members of the pair read aloud at the same time. So, for a few minutes, all the students are simultaneously reading aloud—so there are sometimes rather noisy classes. In the same way that we know that silence is not synonymous with learning (as traditional teaching wanted us to believe), and that silent students may have their mind far away from learning, the noise stemming from peer interaction is not synonymous with learning—not unless it responds to a structure such as we have proposed in the previously described peer tutoring practices: where we might have some noise, but we certainly have learning.

Less discipline problems than anticipated

> When first thinking of implementing peer tutoring in my reading classes, I had serious doubts about giving the most difficult and troublesome students the opportunity to become a tutor. However, I've tried it and I am really surprised about the responsibility they took for their younger tutees and their engagement in and for the project.

We believe this teacher's quote clearly demonstrates teachers' omnipresent fear of losing control during peer tutoring sessions, leading to discipline problems in the reading pairs However, in practice, the fear is usually unfounded when tutors are informed and well prepared for their role.

Within the interaction structure, in the guidance we offer to students telling them what to do during the session, rules of behaviour are implicitly included. The students, in their role as tutors or tutees, try to follow this commitment. So the rules are not seen as external school or teacher standards, but as something necessary for the success of their role. This explains how students with disruptive behaviour in other classes will substantially improve their behaviour in peer tutoring sessions. And when taking up the tutor role, they have opportunities to have their self-esteem boosted, feel some empathy with the teacher, and consequently improve their academic attitudes.

Downplaying the ratio

Peer tutoring sessions break with the traditional concept of ratio of pedagogical assistance, understood as the proportion of aid that each student in the classroom can receive from his or her teacher. For instance, if in a classroom we have a teacher with 28 students, the ratio would be 1:28. But what is the ratio when peer tutoring is used by this teacher? Although this question is complex to answer, we can assume that multiplying the sources of teaching, allows half of the students—the tutees—to receive 1:1 aid. The other half— the tutors—receive 1:14 of teacher support, as well as support provided by tutees in challenging their own learning. The old ratio is downplayed in a classroom in favour of many more adjustable supports available for all.

EMERGENCE OF A NEW ROLE

These changes in the classroom substantially alter the teacher's role in a number of ways.

From transmissive to transformative role

To organise the classroom through peer tutoring, the teacher ceases to perform the traditional role of transmitter of information to all students, with little opportunity for adjusting to the characteristics, preferences or educational needs of each of them. Peer tutoring changes this role to another one, which transforms the classroom into a rich social space with mutual aids. In the role of facilitator and guide, the teacher, however, continues to have a vital and indispensable role in the classroom, requiring careful organisation of interactions between students. The structure acts as a guide for learning, and teacher coaching and guidance of individual pairs adds to this. In the mutual aid processes simultaneously offered by pairs, the teacher can offer tailored aid to the pairs or individuals who require it.

The promotion of autonomy

The interaction structure acts as a pedagogical guide itself, to convert the interaction between tutor and tutee into real learning opportunities. The help of the teacher facilitates progressive transfer of control of the activity to the students. The students, once initially trained in the handling of this structure, work with a high degree of autonomy. In addition, the teacher promotes the necessary reflection in order to encourage student ownership, fitting this structure to the specific needs of the partner. There is a progressive process of transfer of control towards more independent student work. For instance, gradual transfer from external regulation by the teacher to self-regulation of reading strategy use by students is stimulated. Helping students to learn to make their own decisions (autonomy) is an ultimate goal of education.

TEACHING ACTIVITIES

Now let us consider what the main teacher activities are, once the initial training of the students is completed, reading pairs are established and peer tutoring sessions have begun.

FACILITATE AUTONOMOUS WORK IN PAIRS

The teacher needs to provide aid so that the session begins, develops and ends in the most effective way:

■ Ensure pairs are seated in the available spaces side-by-side and provide support material (dictionaries, reading texts, strategy cards, etc.).

■ Resolve attendant issues, such as making alternative arrangements when a student is missing, regrouping pairs, doubling up either tutees or tutors to form threes.

■ Monitor the interaction during the session and progressively transfer time and activity management to pairs. A concrete and visualised step-by-step plan, providing tutors with a scenario of how to keep on track and monitor time, might be a helpful tutor support in this respect.

■ Decorate the class or the places where the pairs are working with items to support the pair work (such as pictograms or visualisations of reading strategies, reading techniques, flow charts, advice on tutor or tutee actions, agreements and compromises, etc.).

■ If pairs are allowed to freely choose books from the class or school library to work on during some of the peer tutoring sessions, make sure there is a wide variety of different types of books and texts (e.g. stories, nonfiction books, magazines, newspapers) that are available and accessible for students. Furthermore, teach children how to choose books autonomously based on their own interest and reading level.

Listen to how students think

While students work in pairs and interact for teaching and learning, the teacher has a unique opportunity to access their minds and to see how they are facing the learning task. Observing and active listening to pairs working allows the teacher to:

■ Gain insight into which resources and strategies students implement to solve the task, improving the teacher's knowledge of them as apprentices and allowing the offering of more adjusted help.

■ Stimulate the ongoing conversation to expand on mechanical responses to questions, to scaffold the student's responses rather than look for the right answer, and to cooperate in the construction of knowledge.

Observe and record the actions of students

During the tutoring sessions, the teacher has time to observe pairs in a planned manner, a few pairs per session or a single behaviour for all of them. This allows:

■ Checking that tutors prepare and responsibly adopt the obligations arising from their role.

- Monitoring the engagement of both members (enthusiasm, attention), the atmosphere (positive rapport, friendly relationship, use of praise) and need for adjustment (extra time, activity adaptation).
- Detecting general or specific training needs of pairs, onward from initial training and concerning the development of role functions, or regarding social skills necessary for cooperative work (e.g. active listening, empathy, reaching compromise agreements, praising the effort of the other). Based on these insights, training needs deserve new consideration in class with respect to optimising the following peer tutoring sessions.

Offer immediate aid

As one teacher commented:

> When first implementing peer tutoring in my daily practice, I did not want to interfere too much in the pairs' collaboration in order to foster and guarantee their autonomy. However, in this respect I missed opportunities for facilitating and improving students' interaction by modelling good helping behaviour, giving examples or asking questions, as well as by providing feedback and praise. Now I realise, the peer tutoring moments are priceless for giving students and pairs immediate support attuned to their needs.

Offer adjusted aid

These selected assistances, responding to tutors or to the pair determined by the teacher, allow quick and efficient adjustment. Thus, the teacher can intervene in pairs in which distraction or a need for support is detected, offering immediate knowledge, clarifications or reminders; or material support, resources and examples. This teaching support will be especially relevant when some students face additional difficulties resulting from unique situations of vulnerability or disability.

Teach social skills

It should not be forgotten that pairs cooperate not only to learn (in this case to improve their reading competence), but also learn to cooperate, which is highly functional learning for the twenty-first century knowledge society. Therefore, the teacher should support students in developing the necessary and complex cooperative social skills. The importance of active listening, clear communication, conflict resolution and agreement should be taken into account.

Use systematic observation as formative assessment

The planned and systematic observation opportunities enabled by peer tutoring sessions should be used to:

- Collect evidence about students' learning, in order to assess their progress. We can use systematic observations of pairs, samplings of tutors' and tutees' work, or an assumed indication of the level of autonomy and quality of the work.

- Encourage self-assessment in the pair and have students demonstrate their own progress (e.g. by periodic recording of tutees reading and analysing their improvement).
- Promote joint reflection on the quality of their performances in their respective roles, through periodic self-assessment guidelines.

Offer feedback

All the above mentioned observation and assessment data on students' and pairs' progress would make little sense if they did not serve to improve teaching and the pairs' activities. Therefore, the teacher should transform such evidence into useful information to support processes of improvement. There are two aspects to this which should be borne in mind.

The first is helping tutors realise that they themselves are learning—improving their own reading competence—through teaching their tutees. Do this by pointing out how preparing materials and offering thoughts and aid allow them to learn. Without the express support of the teacher, it is possible that the student tutor still learns but does not realise it, because of the archaic conception of learning and teaching which argues that the tutee is the only one who is learning.

The second is helping tutees to be aware of the value of peer help and the importance of thanking the tutor for it. But, at the same time, the tutee must attribute the cause of his or her improvement as much to his or her own efforts as to the aid of the tutor, and the peer tutor must also recognise this.

CONCLUSION

In short, the role of the teacher in a peer tutoring project allows the development of actions for quality education. Overcoming the transmissive role, the teacher organises a more democratic classroom where students learn from each other, developing autonomy and social skills. But at the same time, the teacher has the opportunity to develop two actions that normally they cannot. First, observing and listening to their students working—a unique way to know them as learners, since this observation is the basis for continuous formative assessment. And second, offering adjusted and immediate pedagogical aid to those who need it.

13 EVALUATION OF PEER TUTORING

Just because spectacular results have been achieved in some places, that does not guarantee you will get them right where you are. Especially with your first effort, you need to know how successful you have been—and how you can improve effectiveness even more in the future.

Since circumstances will change, or you will want to do something a little differently, so evaluation remains important. Evaluation will also help convince sceptics of the value of what you are doing. Carrying out your own evaluation is a lot more comfortable than some outsider imposing it upon you. You will also find the tutors and tutees very eager to be told how well they have done—so you had better have something concrete to tell them!

One of the great virtues of peer tutoring is its cost-effectiveness. So it would be nonsensical to spend a vast amount of time on evaluation. However, some time is worth devoting to this task. You will need to choose the ways you think are best and easiest for your own situation; but first, you need to think clearly about why you want to do an evaluation.

AIMS AND OBJECTIVES

First, you need to see whether or not your project has been effective. Obviously you want your intervention to have had an effect, and you cannot rely on subjective 'feel-good' factors to evidence this—the school inspectors will not be persuaded by such data! Second, evaluation saves time. Things you have been doing for years (but have never evaluated) are often more difficult to stop than new interventions. Evaluation enables teachers to put their time and effort into the most effective things and avoid approaches that do not work. Third, evaluation guides future action. It takes time, to be sure, but that time is well-invested if it stops you committing a lot more future time in a direction that would not be productive.

So now you need to frame your evaluation question—what is it exactly that you want to find out? Yes, of course you want to know if it 'works'—but with what outcomes, for what groups of students, over what time period, with what frequency? Will you just consider outcomes, or do you want to investigate the nature of the process as well? And what exactly do you mean by 'it'—if peer tutoring is being delivered by different teachers, is it the same in all the classrooms? The evaluation question needs to be as specific as possible if you are to have any hope of measuring it.

EVALUATION DESIGN

The obvious thing is to apply some measure like a reading test at the start of the project and again at the end of the project to assess students' learning gains (i.e. a pre- and post-test design). But if your measure is not norm-referenced (standardised), you will have no way of telling whether the children would have made the pre–post changes anyway, irrespective of the peer tutoring project. Even if your measure is standardised, unless your results are spectacularly better than 'normal' rates of gain, you still will not have evidence that the children could only have made those gains with peer tutoring. Moreover, reading is taught in almost all subjects. Without a control group, you cannot be sure whether the gains in reading are due to the project.

So you really need to compare the progress of your project children with the progress of a similar group who have not been involved in the project—a 'control' or 'comparison' group. This is called a *pre–posttest control group design*. A true control group is identical to the experimental group (i.e. the group of children involved in the peer tutoring project) in every way (including pretest attainment, age or gender balance). Random allocation to experimental or control groups is often suggested to be the most scientific way of equalising the two groups. However, with small numbers, random allocation sometimes yields groups that are not actually identical. Also, few tutoring organisers find it very practical.

However you organise the experimental and control groups, you also need to think about how they are in fact different. Do they have different teachers, for instance? Or do the classes meet at different times of day, when one might be more tired than the other? Do the two classes spend different amounts of time-on-task at reading? If one class is reading more than the other (irrespective of how they are doing it) you might expect the class with more reading to improve. Did the experimental class teacher choose to be involved in the project, while the control group teacher did not really care? If one of your teachers self-selected to participate, they are likely to be more highly motivated to make the project succeed than would be the case if they had not.

One of the problems with control groups is that their use seems to involve denying a service or facility to people who are in need of it, at least in the short run. You can justify this on the grounds that you do not have the resources to effectively help everyone all at the same time and besides, random allocation is fairer than other methods of 'rationing'. It can also be argued that until you have demonstrated that the project has actually worked by using the control group, you don't know whether you are denying the control group anything worthwhile. Furthermore, comparison groups are probably only necessary in the first phases of your project. If the results are positive you perhaps do not need to use a comparison group in the future.

Alternatively, think about a *time series* or *baseline design*. For instance, if a school has a regular routine of applying reading tests, historical data some time in the past may be available for the project group. This enables you to scrutinise the fluctuations in progress in the past, and see how the gains during the project compare. In a sense, each person serves as their own control over time. Where the regular trend of time series data is 'interrupted' by a special event like a peer tutoring project, you check to see what sort of a blip in the trend emerges. You could even combine a control/comparison group with a baseline/time series, giving a *baseline or time series with comparison series*. It is certainly advantageous if the time series can be continued after the end of the project; this will generate very interesting and valuable long-term follow-up data.

One further design is probably worth mentioning here—the *multiple baseline design*. If a larger group of potential clients exists than can be serviced at one time, they may have to be serviced by two consecutive projects. Where one half of the clients has to be serviced first, and the second later, it is reasonable and fair to allocate students to 'early' and 'late' groups randomly.

Teachers will often do this when a whole class of (say) 30 wants to do peer tutoring, but it is clear that there is not enough teacher time to look at 30 diary cards each week. It is better to work with half of the class properly at one time, rather than overload and stress the system. The 'late' group will be all the more enthusiastic for having their appetite whetted. Quite often the late group makes bigger gains than the 'early' group!

So in the short term, you compare the gains of the participant early group to those of the nonparticipant late comparison group. In the medium term, you compare the gains of the now participant late group to their own progress before participating, and to the progress of the early group when participating. Or you can collect postparticipation follow-up data on the early group, and compare those to their own gains while participating. In the longer term, you can collect postparticipation follow-up data on the late group and compare those to the follow-up data on the early group, as well as to their own participation gains. You can also collect longer follow-up data on the early group and compare those to their shorter follow-up data. Try drawing these on a graph of time against reading test scores.

Whatever evaluation design you choose to apply, think about the possibility of the 'Hawthorne Effect'. This effect unfolds when participants in a study show brief improvement purely because some attention is being paid to them and there is some element of novelty about the proceedings, quite irrespective of the actual nature of the intervention. For the experimental group, this possibility makes follow-up important. It might also account for unexpected gains in the control group.

Another possible source of embarrassment is the 'John Henry Effect'—where the control group, alerted to the fact that somebody considers them to be in need but is not providing anything for them, consciously determines to improve anyway, and does so without apparent outside intervention.

TYPES OF EVALUATION

There are two main types of evaluation: summative (or outcome or product) evaluation; and formative (or process) evaluation.

Summative evaluation looks solely at the end-product or outcome of a peer tutoring project, such as gains in reading skills.

Formative evaluation looks closely at how effective each of the various aspects of the organisation and methods of the peer tutoring project were in achieving this goal (for example, training quality, attendance rates, technique compliance). Formative evaluation enables you to re-form a better project next time, or even adjust the current one as you go along.

As has been documented in previous chapters, peer tutoring allows the teacher to engage in activities that are difficult to do in more traditional classes. One of these activities is continuous evaluation. These data can be used not only as a student summative assessment, but also as a formative evaluation. For instance, in the PR project, data could include plans on the Planning Proforma (see eResources website), checked against subsequent reality, collected observations on a technique checklist, and collected diaries. It could include any other observations and opinions collected from any participants about the project as you go along. An 'independent' observer to record observations in situ can be very helpful, but takes time and resources. This is even truer of video or audio recordings of a few pairs during each session—you will find it very difficult to find time to analyse the recordings. The effect of the presence of the observer, especially in small group settings, also has to be taken into account.

Very often, evaluations focus too much on before and after measurements. This fails to capture the complexity of what has happened during the project. You will want to know how well the intervention has been implemented (termed 'implementation integrity' or 'implementation fidelity') in order to set the outcome results in that context. Obviously, for a weakly implemented intervention, you would not expect such good results as for a strongly implemented evaluation. You may of course find changes over time in implementation integrity—as in projects which started out well, but became weaker over time as the novelty wore off or the teacher was changed. Others may struggle at the start but get better as time goes on.

The section on 'Measures' below inevitably focuses mainly on project end-products, although some of the methods discussed throw some tangential light on processes involved.

MEASURES

There are various basic requirements of any measurement instruments you use. Economy of cost in materials and of time in administration and scoring are two obvious considerations. The measure needs to be reliable, in the sense of not being susceptible to wild random fluctuations or erratic guesswork. It also needs to be valid—that is, one must be assured that it actually measures what it is claiming to measure. Of equal importance, it needs to be relevant to the processes in question—it needs to measure things of value, not just things which are easy to measure.

Last, but by no means least, the measure must generate information which is analysable. A vast quantity of impressionistic opinion or observation data may be fascinating to the project organisers, but will not enable them to communicate their findings to others in a brief, clear and credible way. These considerations are worth bearing in mind irrespective of the type(s) of measure chosen, which we can now consider.

Teachers are often inclined to use national assessments (which are already being conducted in the school anyway) as measures in a project. The problem here is that such measures are often too vague to be sufficiently discriminatory when used for such a purpose. Where the test is conducted by the teacher running the project, there is also the 'halo' effect of positivity resulting from the teacher having invested energy and being determined to see a positive outcome. Such tests are also not very reliable when conducted by different teachers.

Standardised tests from reputable suppliers may be more discriminatory—able to detect fine differences in performance—but of course, cost money. If the school is not already using them anyway, it may be difficult to persuade the head teacher to purchase them.

Then there is the possibility of designing your own tests—which sounds cheaper but actually costs a lot of teacher time. You will then have the problem that the reliability of the test you have designed may well be suspect.

Remember that children almost always progress over time, whether they have received any intervention or not, as a result of maturation and the overall effect of schooling and learning at home or elsewhere. Consequently, you need to make sure that your measure allows for this (e.g. by relating performance on each occasion of testing to chronological age on each occasion) or that it is taken into account by the use of a control or comparison group.

Individual versus group tests

Reading tests administered individually to children, rather than group tests, might give a more valid indication of how well the child can actually read—unless they are very brief or the content is restricted to a single narrow kind of reading. Reading to a real person sitting next to you is also much more like the peer tutoring experience. Even if one child does not respond well and seems inattentive and unmotivated, at least you can see that, and interpret the results accordingly. However, administering one individual test after the other takes far more time than administering a group test to the whole group or class.

Group tests are much quicker to administer (although you still have to find time to score each one), but despite carefully watching the group of children during testing, you will be much less certain whether a child's score really reflects his or her reading ability. You might be especially careful about giving individual results on group tests to parents or students, since the individual results might not be very reliable, although the overall group means might be. Individual scores might fluctuate implausibly, even though the group averages seem about right.

This dilemma of choice seems likely to be—to some extent—resolved in well-resourced countries by the increasing introduction of adaptive computer-based assessment of reading skills. This involves each child testing individually at the computer in turn, with immediate automatic scoring by the computer. The test content is adaptively individualised to the child, so testing is brief and stress is limited; and children are generally highly motivated, although the personal interaction element is missing.

Norm-referenced versus criterion-referenced tests

Some tests are standardised (also known as norm-referenced). This means that the performance of a great many children on the test has been analysed to see what constitutes the 'normal' range of performance for children of different ages. Each new child's performance can then be compared to these 'norms'. Most of such tests are only available commercially and have to be purchased.

Curriculum-based or criterion-referenced tests are different—they check to see whether the child has or has not attained a certain level or criterion of performance on materials very close to (or maybe drawn from) the curriculum the child is following. If you use such a test with a group of children, you will of course get some idea of what is 'normal' for your group. Some criterion-referenced tests are available commercially, many are available free of charge (increasingly on the internet), and many are devised by schools or individual teachers for their own purposes.

At first sight, criterion-referenced tests seem more attractive. They are likely to be cheaper and more closely related to what the child has actually done (which is to be evaluated), and probably less likely to frighten or distress the weaker student.

However, information on reliability and validity tends to be much sparser with crite-rion-referenced than with standardised tests. Good results on standardised tests might be harder to obtain, but are likely to be more persuasive, because such tests are assess-ing generalisation of improved skills to completely new material and new situations. Furthermore, you need to check if the samples used for the standardisation of the test really represent the whole country. Are they likely to represent your students? Look for a relatively recent standardisation or restandardisation, perhaps in a new edition. Of course, in many countries standardised tests of reading are not available, so criterion-referenced tests are the only option.

Test reliability and validity

The manuals for tests should contain detailed information about their reliability and validity. You should check for this information in the test manual. You may find this information is inadequate or missing, in which case avoid the test. Even if it is there and reassuringly positive, remember that average reliability and validity with a normal dis-tribution of children might not necessarily be the same as the reliability and validity you actually obtain with your small and idiosyncratic group of children.

Where standardised or criterion-referenced tests are in use, pre- and postproject mea-sures should be carried out by the same person, to ensure that any peculiarities of admin-istration or any bias (particularly to generosity in scoring) or other 'tester effects' will be the same on both occasions.

Test range

If your readers (experimental and control) are of a wide range of reading ability, make sure the test you choose covers this range. Remember that at posttest, performance and chronological age will be higher, and this will be even truer at follow-up. Beware of tests which will suffer from a 'ceiling' or 'floor' effect (i.e. no discrimination, or maybe no scores at all, for very able or less able readers, or very young or old readers). So children with a high pretest score have little scope to better it; while at the other extreme, many children may be given the same very low (or 'below scale') score at posttest when they are actually quite different in reading competence. On the other hand, if the test is very long, in order to include many items at all levels of difficulty, it will be very oppressive for the weaker readers, whose self-esteem might be damaged by testing.

Also watch for calibration effects—some tests include many items covering the middle part of the total span they claim to cover, but have very few items at the extremes. So at the extremes, getting just one more item right or wrong could make a big difference to the standardised performance score.

Test content and aim

Some tests that are still available were created long ago and have very dated content— perhaps words, ideas or events that are no longer common. Older tests (and some of the newer ones) can have a strong cultural bias—often favouring the white middle-class child who speaks the school language as their first language. Look for words, events or ideas that might be currently common in some cultural groups, but are not in others. This can distort the test results.

As mentioned above, very brief tests and/or those with content restricted to a single narrow kind of reading with very limited context are unlikely to be satisfactory. Look for tests that give a reading experience somewhat like real reading—at least passages of continuous meaningful prose.

Consider if the test is really only measuring accuracy of decoding, or whether it is also assessing comprehension. The latter is highly desirable, of course, especially if the peer tutoring project aims to foster comprehension. Consider whether it can assess comprehension only if decoding accuracy is good. Does it also measure speed or rate of reading? This latter might not, however, be very important, since for some children reading slower is actually an improvement.

Test practice effects

If children do better at posttest than at pretest, might it just be because they have remembered some of the answers, and therefore have more energy to attack the harder items? This would be a 'content practice effect' on a repeat test with the same content. Even if the posttest had different test items, children would be familiar with the format, and might do better owing to that (a 'format practice effect'). Both of these are reasons for using a control group, for whom any practice effects would be the same.

Practice effects are not always positive, however. Children might be bored with the test at its second encounter, and consequently unmotivated. Think about the time of year you do the test and the conditions under which it is done. Was one occasion when the children were near the end of the school session or year and thus not motivated? Was it very rushed on one occasion? If it is a very long test, and they know they struggled with a majority of the items at first encounter, they might give up completely right from the start at the second measurement occasion.

Where tests are available in parallel forms (to limit content practice effects, if not format practice effects), check carefully that the parallel forms are actually equivalent. Sometimes they are not. To guard against this possibility, you can allocate test forms to children by occasion—so one child has form A at pretest and form B at posttest, while the child sitting next to him or her has it the other way round. This also helps reduce the possibility of copying answers, a potential problem with group test administration in a crowded classroom.

Informal reading inventories

An Informal Reading Inventory (IRI) is a kind of curriculum-based test, but its use may be particular to certain countries. It is based on a series of passages of increasing complexity taken from typical reading material in the real life context, carefully graded for difficulty, with associated comprehension questions. Readability could be assessed through one of the standard formulae, now available as computer programs for scanned text, or the passages could be systematically drawn from some prelevelled material, such as basal readers or a reading laboratory. The student is asked to read the passages in order of increasing difficulty until they reach their frustration level. Independence level is defined as 99% accuracy, 90% comprehension; instructional level as 95% accuracy, 75% comprehension; and frustration level as 90% or less accuracy, 50% or less comprehension. While the student is reading, a practised tester can also note the nature of the errors made, allowing subsequent diagnostic error analysis (or 'miscue' analysis).

Unfortunately, IRIs are time-consuming to devise and to individually administer; however, they are much more like 'real' reading.

Cloze tests

An alternative possibility is some kind of Cloze test, again based on curriculum materials in a sequence of ascending difficulty. A series of passages are reproduced with some words deleted. The deletions can be of a predominantly syntactic or semantic nature, a combination of both or be random. The children have to supply the missing words. If the exercise is done on a silent reading basis, which is the more common, no emphasis is placed on spelling correctness in the child's insertions. The disadvantages of IRIs are shared by Cloze tests. Cloze tests on a silent reading basis involve less actual time expenditure by the tester, but yield less useful information. Some commercial standardised tests use a Cloze structure.

High frequency words

Especially with young, emergent or delayed readers, finding any test with a low enough 'floor' and sufficient discrimination to register any improvement might be difficult. A possibility is to construct a word recognition test from the Dolch, Edwards or more recent lists of the most commonly occurring (high frequency) words. Much the same exercise could be carried out using items of vocabulary from the school's core basal reading scheme. Scoring could be in terms of number of words read correctly out of a given set of words, or in terms of how many words the child could read correctly in a given time span. There are different views about whether reading faster is necessarily a good thing, but speeded tests may be worth a try as a measure of fluency on vocabulary which should be familiar. Of course, how reading isolated words relates to the contextualised reading that characterises the PR process is questionable.

Attitude to and motivation for reading

In addition to administering reading tests for measuring reading accuracy or comprehension, teachers might also consider assessing motivational effects of the peer tutoring project. In this respect, a variety of 'attitude to reading' scales are available, but many are long and complex paper and pencil exercises of doubtful relevance and limited specificity, quite apart from the considerations of reliability and validity. The Elementary Reading Attitude Survey (McKenna & Kear, 1990; McKenna, Kear & Ellsworth, 1995) uses a Garfield cartoon character which appeals to young children. Also in the public domain is the Motivation To Read Profile (Gambrell, Palmer, Codling & Mazzoni, 1996) or the recently developed SRQ-Reading Motivation (De Naeghel, Van Keer, Vansteenkiste & Rosseel, 2012).

Self-concept scales

The socioemotional aspects of peer tutoring are highly significant, and attempts can be made to tap these by some form of measure. Some group 'tests' of self-concept are available, and in some cases these are subdivided into 'academic self-concept' and other areas of self-concept. Single tests specifically of reading self-concept are rare, but the Reader

Self-Perception Scale (Henk & Melnick, 1995) is one that is available in the public domain. The complexity and intangibility of the socioemotional factors involved render them difficult to reveal on paper and pencil measures.

SUBJECTIVE FEEDBACK

The subjective views of the major participants in the project (tutees, parent tutors, peer tutors, volunteer tutors and teachers) should always be elicited in some way. To rely simply on instruments such as tests is to risk missing the texture of the reality of what happened. The participants will probably offer more process insights than summative conclusions, but the former must not be neglected. Formulating and communicating opinions serves not only to gather information, but also to clarify the participant's mind on the subject, resolve any residual practical problems and, very often, to recharge and commit the participants to continued effort.

A group meeting for all participants at the end of the initial period is often a good idea. This could be (audio or video) tape-recorded for more detailed analysis later (although the analysis could prove a massive task). If time is available, individual interviews with at least some of the participants along some semistructured format is desirable. Similar interviews with the teachers are also desirable, but probably need carrying out by an 'outsider' to the project if they are to be remotely objective.

Realistically, time constraints and/or the need to have readily analysable data often drive people into using some form of structured questionnaire. However, there are very large doubts about the reliability and validity of responses to questionnaires, even supposing you obtain a high response rate, and other forms of data gathering should be carried out as well. The kind of superficial subjective feedback gathered by questionnaires might be particularly susceptible to the 'grateful testimonials effect'. Your respondents know you have worked hard, think you are a nice person, and do not want to tell you anything except what they think you want to hear. If the response rate to your questionnaire is low, it is even more likely that the returns will be biased positively.

In the construction of questionnaires, the project leaders or participants are best placed to decide which questions are important to them. However, the questionnaire must be structured to eliminate any possibility of leading respondents into giving a particular answer. A multiple-choice format gives easily analysable data, but is crude and simplistic; while an open-ended format is dependent on the free writing skills of the respondents and yields data which are often difficult to analyse. Where a self-designed questionnaire is used, you should 'pilot' it with a relevant subgroup in your own locality first.

If you want people's feelings about the project, ask for them directly, but do not expect them necessarily to bear much relationship to the participants' actual behaviour or even the children's progress in reading. On the other hand, if you want observations of what participants actually did, ask for that directly, giving a 'no observations made' option. But avoid confusing the two.

Reproducible specimen questionnaires can be found on the eResources website in different language versions. These include questionnaires for parent tutors, peer tutors, tutees (irrespective of tutor) and teachers or other project organisers (with respect to individual children or the whole class/group). These have the advantage of previous widespread use, the results from which can be considered to form a crude kind of 'standardisation' or norm-reference (for example, see Topping & Whiteley, 1990).

These questionnaires have been carefully constructed to avoid leading the respondents into 'yea-saying'. Thus, even if you feel the exact questions are not relevant to your context, you might wish to reflect upon the structure. If you are able to conduct individual interviews, specimen interview schedules are also available on the eResources website, which should give ideas for a peer tutoring interview schedule.

ANALYSIS OF DATA

There is a great difference between statistical and educational significance. The larger your sample, the more likely you are to obtain statistical significance, other things being equal. So big gains for your tutors and tutees compared to a control group may not be statistically significant if you only have five children in each group. On the other hand, if a very large tutoring project produces gains in the project group which, compared to those in the control group, are only just statistically significant, searching questions need asking about the educational significance of the results. Was it worth all that time and effort for gains so small? Do other gains that are perhaps more difficult to measure (e.g. social and communicative skills and attitudes) justify this effort?

Especially with smaller samples, you might want to calculate the effect size rather than rely on statistical significance. This has the advantage of enabling you to compare with other projects more easily. Assuming both intervention and control groups had similar average pretest results, take the average posttest score of the experimental group and subtract the average posttest score of the control group; then divide by the standard deviation of the control group. The resulting figure can be classified as small if it is around 0.2, moderate if it is around 0.5 and large if it is around 0.8.

It should also be borne in mind that where a very large number of different outcome measures are used, there is a chance that one or two will show statistically significant changes irrespective of any real impact of the project (with the attendant risk of assuming the intervention has worked when in fact it has not—what is known as Type 1 error). Fortunately, peer tutoring projects do not usually find themselves in this area of doubt, since the majority of moderately well-organised projects show gains of at least twice 'normal' rates of progress, and the educational significance of this is rarely in doubt, even before more subjective feedback is considered.

For those unsure of their competence in statistical analysis, or doubting the validity of statistical analysis, simple comparison of raw data in tables or on scattergrams or other graphs of shifts in averages for groups gives a ready visual indication of changes.

If you really want to do some statistical analysis, before you can decide whether to use parametric or nonparametric statistical analysis, you need to consider:

■ The level of measurement of your measures
■ The size of your samples
■ The nature of your sampling framework
■ The nature of the comparisons you wish to make (within or between groups).

Then, consult a statistics textbook or one of the public domain online internet tutorials (a web search engine will find the current ones). If you do not understand what the things are that you need to consider, you definitely need to consult a statistics textbook.

EVALUATION RESULTS FEEDBACK

One of the disadvantages of complex data analysis is that it takes time, and very often early feedback of evaluation results to the project participants is highly desirable, to renew their commitment and recharge their energies. A simple graph and/or brief tables of average scores for the groups are probably the best vehicle for this—remember, the results must be understood by the youngest tutees as well.

Keep in mind that the purpose of evaluation is to know the effect of your tutoring programme on your students' learning. But at the same time it is very important that it provides you with relevant information about how you can improve it. How can you reduce the weak points and get better results?

Evaluation results have a number of other uses as well. Publicity—via the local press, professional journals, education curriculum bulletins or in-service meetings—not only helps to disseminate good practice and aid more children, it also serves to boost the morale of the project initiators and participants.

The results may be useful to convince sceptics on the school staff, generate a wider interest and produce a more coherent future policy on parent involvement in the school. The school board of governors will be interested, as should be various school district or state officers. A demonstration of cost-effectiveness may elicit more tangible support from administration or politicians. Associated services, such as children's library services and reading and language centres, might be drawn into the network of community support by a convincing evaluation report.

So to the final word. If you get results you don't like, you'll spend hours puzzling over them trying to explain them away. Make sure that if you do get results you do like, you spend as much time and energy searching for other factors outside the project that could have produced them. If you don't spot them, someone else might—and probably will!

14 SUSTAINING AND EMBEDDING PEER TUTORING

Education suffers greatly from short-lived initiatives which enjoy a brief period of being fashionable, then fall out of favour and disappear without trace. It is worrying that some of these initiatives seem to become fashionable even though there is no good evidence for their effectiveness. It is even more worrying that some seem to go out of fashion even when there is good evidence that they are effective.

So, you have successfully completed a first peer tutoring project. You have seen worthwhile improvement in a majority of your students, and are feeling pleased with yourself. Great! Now it is time to think about consolidation—embedding peer tutoring within the school organisation so that it continues to maximise student potential, enduring through whatever political, financial, sociological or other tides that might flow your way—and preferably making it so widespread, durable and embedded in the system that it will endure long after you have left the school.

With the intention of successful consolidation, we discuss some important considerations and points to bear in mind below.

OBJECTIVES, APPLICATIONS AND EVALUATION

When embedding peer tutoring in the school organisation, you need to continue to be clear about the different objectives for different types of peer tutoring. Your objectives for a specific project might be in the cognitive, affective or social domains—or some combination of these. Make sure you agree within the school team on the objectives you want to pursue. Don't let someone else evaluate your project against a different set of objectives!

As to the different possible applications, consider using a mixture of cross-age and same-age, cross-ability and same-ability, fixed-role and reciprocal-role peer tutoring as necessary and optimal to achieve your objectives.

Plan for flexibility. If you work at it you can figure out a peer tutoring format or method which will fit into almost any local exigencies: complex organisations, highly structured schedules, lack of physical space, lack of appropriate furniture, poor acoustics, rigid attitudes in adults in positions of power, rigid attitudes in children who have learned to prefer passive inertia, and so on. But don't be too ambitious to start with—many small steps get you there quickest in the end.

Finally, after defining your objectives and deciding on the peer tutoring formats to embed, choose your evaluation format and design accordingly to suit your context, objectives and possibilities. Consider which formats will suit which subjects, topics, activities, classes, and so on.

Projects must target and evaluate gains for all participants (particularly the tutors). Feeding general data on their success back to the participants might well increase their longer-term motivation. Publicising the data might expand subsequent recruitment or attract additional funding. But how will you review to what extent the curriculum content of the activity has actually been mastered and retained in the longer term?

In this respect, evaluation should seek to check whether there are longer-term as well as short-term gains. You will need to build in some means for continuing review, feedback and injection of further novelty and enthusiasm. Otherwise, all pairs will not automatically keep going and maintain the use of their skills. And the same goes for the teachers involved in the project. Furthermore, evidence on the generalisation of gains in other contexts and other curriculum areas outside the specifically nominated peer tutoring sessions is also important. You are likely to need to consciously foster participants in broadening the use of their new skills to different materials and contexts for new purposes. All of this will consolidate the progress made, build confidence and empower the pairs still further.

MATERIALS, METHODS AND MONITORING

Materials should preferably be low cost, already to hand, differentiated for different needs, attractive and durable. A simple system for access to and exchange of the necessary materials is needed. Tracking current student possession of materials might be necessary, but don't get hung up with bureaucracy that creates extra work. One might also think of giving tutors responsibility for keeping an overview or list of materials.

Prescribe a clear and simple method for peer interaction to start with. Ensure the participants always receive good quality training in this respect and understand the basis of peer tutoring and its benefits for themselves. Particularly, tutors have to know that they themselves can learn by teaching their tutees. Remember, methods need to be truly and consistently interactive—or (at least) one partner will go to sleep and lose motivation and engagement. Ensure the method involves modelling as well as much discussion, questioning and explaining. Ensure there are clear procedures for the identification, diagnosis and correction of errors. Make certain that tutors engage in praise and constructive feedback when relevant.

Taking into account all the above, you create important prerequisites for fruitful interaction, guaranteeing that the method builds in and capitalises on intrinsic satisfaction for all participants. Once the participants are experiencing success, ensure they do not become dependent on a routine method, and make clear the times and opportunities within which they are encouraged and even required to be creative and take the initiative to add to the suggested method for peer interaction. When tutors and tutees have developed sufficient awareness of effective tutoring to begin to design their own systems, you know you have done a good job. You might find peer tutoring popping up when you least expect it, driven by the students themselves.

Close monitoring of participant behaviour is especially necessary at the beginning, where student deviation can lead to failure. Students need time to learn to play their respective roles. After an initial period of 'getting it right', creative and reflective deviance in students might be encouraged, but will need close monitoring. In the longer run, some 'drift' is almost inevitable—keep checking to see that it is productive and reflect on this with the students to optimise future peer tutoring sessions.

REJUVENATION AND ITERATION

Initiating a project (especially in an inert environment) is very demanding in terms of time and energy, although that capital investment is almost always considered worthwhile later. Once things are up and running smoothly, it is tempting to either relax, or rush on and start another project with a different group. The latter is more dangerous than the former—don't spread yourself too thinly. After a few weeks or months, most initiatives need some rejuvenation—not necessarily an organisational improvement, just a change to inject some novelty and provide your project with new oxygen.

Fortunately, peer tutoring is very flexible and offers many ways for injecting variety and novelty—change of partners, subject topics or activities, format of operation, and so on. However, please do not try to use it for everything, or you will overdose the learners. It can enhance productivity to give them a rest for a certain period and then return to a modified format not too long afterwards. In any event, close consultation with the students always adds extra momentum to their motivation—even if their suggestions are contradictory and cannot all be implemented, the feeling that their views are valued increases commitment to the onward process.

You might wish to consider to what extent you can give away some of the organisation and management to the participants themselves. Obviously, you would need to check on this from time to time, especially with younger children. Of course, you would wish positives to be accentuated and negatives to be eliminated. In this respect, keeping the feel-good factor going is important. However, a degree of self-management (which can include self-monitoring) can heighten self-esteem and responsibility and help to make initiatives self-sustaining.

Once peer tutoring is accepted and deployed by more staff, some coordination will be necessary. Working together, you can build iterative cycles of involvement in different kinds of peer tutoring in different formats with all children in both roles, as tutors and tutees at different times, in a developmental, progressive sequence.

A WARNING ABOUT CUSTOMISATION

Teachers know best about their own schools and teaching conditions. And all methods explained in this book need adjustments to the local characteristics. Enthusiastic teachers often want to customise or adapt methods, to 'suit' their own classroom or children. The materials on the eResources website are deliberately made available electronically, so that they can be customised to local needs. However, a word of warning is needed: it is only the structured methods described here that have been evaluated. If you customise so enthusiastically that your method no longer bears much relationship to the original, you cannot expect automatic transfer of effectiveness. For all of these reasons, we suggest that—at least for your first venture into this field—you keep to the guidelines outlined in this book (which still needs you to make many professional decisions about what is best for your own class and your own children).

EXTENDING IN ALL DIRECTIONS

In addition to embedding peer tutoring as part of continuing mainstream practice, you will wish to consider extending it:

- ■ To more tutors and tutees
- ■ To tutors and tutees with greater difficulties
- ■ To other subject areas
- ■ To other classes and colleagues
- ■ To other peer tutoring methods
- ■ To involve parents or volunteers
- ■ To collaborate with another school.

The potential is enormous. But as ever, remember that a modest development done well is better than a large development done badly.

REACHING THE HARD-TO-REACH

In peer tutoring programmes, the raw material (students) is always to hand (except for children who truant—but even they often turn up for their peer tutoring session).

You need to feel persuaded that the mass of previous research data on the effectiveness of peer tutoring are relevant to your project. You need to find that your own local evaluation gives you positive results. Then the first students to experience the intervention will probably like it—and will be passing the word on to their younger brothers and sisters and other younger students, who will be expecting this to be available to them as they move up the school. Before long, you may find that demand for the intervention is more than you can easily cope with, and that the students are more universally positive than the remaining nonparticipant teachers.

Many teachers will be worried about the neediest children, whether their neediness arises from a continuing learning disability or from a more transient language learning problem. Will such children be able to cope with peer tutoring, either as tutees or indeed as tutors? Sometimes teachers are tempted to exclude such children from a project and have them work with adult helpers instead. We recommend, however, not going for the latter. *All* children should have the opportunity to participate in and benefit from peer tutoring; even a pair with a weak tutor working with a weak tutee can learn! The fact that the pair is required to interact will certainly place demands upon them, and these demands will help them to learn.

DEVELOPING A WHOLE-SCHOOL APPROACH

There is no better apprenticeship for being a tutor than being a tutee. Many schools with cross-year class-wide peer tutor programmes actively promote the equal opportunity and apprenticeship advantages of this model. Every student who is helped in a lower grade fully expects from the outset to become a tutor when in a higher grade. As students are helped in preparation for becoming helpers, any ambivalence about receiving help decreases and motivation to learn often increases. The asymmetry between tutor and tutee is reduced, and the stigma often otherwise associated with receiving help disappears.

All the students have the chance to participate and the opportunity to help, which makes them all feel equally valuable and worthwhile.

Sometimes, students who are helped in one subject are simultaneously helpers to students in a lower grade in the same subject. Those who are helped in one subject might be helpers to their own age peers in another subject. Even the most able student in any grade can be presented with problems that require the help of an even more capable student from a higher grade, and thereby learn that no one is as smart as all of us. The symbiosis of the tutor and tutee roles is something upon which to consciously capitalise.

Over time, a critical mass of teachers who support peer tutoring can develop in the school. Peer tutoring builds on students' strengths and mobilises them as active participants in the learning process. Not only do helpers learn the subject better and deeper, but they also learn transferable skills in helping and cooperation, listening and communication. All of this influences the school ethos, developing a cultural norm of helping and caring. Peer tutoring contributes to a sense of cohesive community and encourages personal and social development. Eventually, it can permeate the whole ethos of a school and be deployed spontaneously in many areas of the curriculum—a learning tool as natural as opening a book or turning on a computer. When you see your students explaining to a newcomer from another school or district what peer tutoring is all about, and showing amazement on discovering that not everybody does it everywhere, you will know you have it embedded. Something that began as an innovation has become a regular methodology!

SHARE THE PROJECT WITH OTHER TEACHERS

Although every working day they are part of a very busy community, teachers all too often feel strangely isolated. Finding time together to have a discussion about anything is difficult enough—and at the end of the school day, energies are at low ebb for professional discussions. Ideally, time should be scheduled to bring teachers together regularly in mutual support and problem-solving gatherings where they can share their ideas, materials and methods—and build up each other's confidence and self-esteem. Peer tutoring works very well with teachers, too! Teachers can learn from each other by sharing their experiences in implementing an innovative practice. Maybe a first step in this direction could be inviting some colleagues to your peer tutoring session, and then asking their opinion.

Peer tutoring allows teachers to put groups together and co-teach with other teachers, as well as to plan, support and evaluate students jointly. If students see their teachers working together—sharing responsibilities in class—they will understand better why they have to collaborate with their peers. If the responsibility of the peer tutoring programme is shared between several teachers, the programme will have more opportunities to become sustainable over the years and become a regular method in the school. And, of course, this is the goal.

Keeping in touch with other schools that use peer tutoring could be another good resource. If they are in the same geographical area, maybe teachers can visit each other's school and observe peer tutoring sessions, to learn how other colleagues do it. An exchange of experiences between students could be interesting too. If schools are not near, you can use the internet and create a network to share the projects and learn from each other. This is a sort of peer learning too, when the peers are whole schools as well as individuals.

ENSURING SUSTAINED SUCCESS

How are we to ensure the longer-term success of peer tutoring strategies? Embedding peer tutoring within an organisation or larger community requires careful attention to the needs of the learners, the parents, the professional educators and the wider system. In order for a peer tutoring initiative to last and grow, there are some considerations that should be met.

First, the benefits must outweigh the costs for all concerned if the initiative is to endure. For the initiating teacher, costs will be in terms of time devoted, materials and other resources, and the general harassment and stress involved in doing anything new. All of these must be kept as low as possible. On the benefit side, the teacher will need both subjective and objective evidence of *impact* in relation to the objectives of the peer tutoring project set. Sometimes we have a lot of *cold* data about project success (test results, questionnaires, etc.), but the subjective data are not always easy to gather. Find ways to allow for enthusiastic children to express their satisfaction, after being tutors or tutees—happiness in learning is one of the teacher's goals, after all. More than that, the whole initiative also has to feel good—have a warm and satisfying social and emotional tone—and this will benefit from a little deliberate cultivation.

Parental involvement in the peer tutoring project is highly necessary. This is true not only in order so that the parents understand the method, and how their sons or daughters learn to play the role of tutor or tutee; but also because if they are well informed, and have opportunities to visit the sessions or to take part in them, they will value the project and will be another active support for ensuring its sustained success.

No teacher is an island, and the initiative also needs to be compatible with the current local philosophy, political correctness and mood of the professional peer group and senior policy-makers. Fortunately, peer tutoring has largely escaped adverse politicisation—it is right up there with motherhood and apple pie in terms of acceptability.

A similar analysis can be applied to the other participants—the tutors, the tutees and the head of the institution. They also need minimisation of time wastage and harassment, need to feel good about the project, need to be clear what they are getting out of it and what the other participants are getting out of it, and need to be able to confidently assert their support for it in the face of incredulity from their own peer group.

REFERENCES

Aarnoutse, C. & Schellings, G. (2003). Learning reading strategies by triggering reading motivation. *Educational Studies, 29*(4), 387–409.

Almasi, J. F. & Garas-York, K. (2009). Comprehension and discussion of text. In S. Israel & G. Duffy (Eds), *Handbook of research on reading comprehension* (pp. 470–493). New York: Routledge.

Al-Momani, I. A., Ihmeideh, F. M. & Naba'h, A. M. A. (2010). Teaching reading in the early years: Exploring home and kindergarten relationships. *Early Child Development and Care, 180*(6), 767–785.

Alvermann, D. E. (2000). Classroom talk about texts: Is it dear, cheap or a bargain at any price? In B. M. Taylor, M. F. Graves & P. Van den Broek (Eds), *Reading for meaning: Fostering comprehension in the middle grades* (pp. 170–192). New York: Teachers College Press.

Alvermann, D. E., Fitzgerald, J. & Simpson, M. (2006). Teaching and learning in reading. In P. A. Alexander & P. H. Wine (Eds), *Handbook of educational psychology* (pp. 427–455). Mahwah, NJ: Lawrence Erlbaum Associates.

Ashwin, P. (2003). Peer support: Relations between the context, process, and outcomes for the students who are supported. *Instructional Science, 31*, 159–173.

Azevedo, R. & Hadwin, A. F. (2005). Scaffolding self-regulated learning and metacognition: Implications for the design of computer-based scaffolds. *Instructional Science, 33*, 367–379.

Baker, D. L., Park, Y., Baker, S. K., Basaraba, D. L., Kame'enui, E. J. & Beck, C. T. (2012). Effects of a paired bilingual reading programme and an English-only programme on the reading performance of English learners in grades 1–3. *Journal of School Psychology, 50*(6), 737–758.

Bell, K. & Caspari, A. (2002). *Strategies for improving non-fiction reading comprehension.* ERIC Accession Number ED471787.

Bentz, J. L. & Fuchs, L. S. (1996). Improving peers' helping behavior to students with learning disabilities during mathematics peer tutoring. *Learning Disability Quarterly, 19*, 202–215.

Blanch, S., Duran, D., Valdebenito, V. & Flores, M. (2013). The effects and characteristics of family involvement on a peer tutoring programme to improve the reading comprehension competence. *European Journal of Psychology Education, 28*(1), 101–119.

Block, C., Parris, S., Reed, L., Whiteley, C. & Cleveland, M. (2009). Instructional approaches that significantly increase reading comprehension. *Journal of Educational Psychology, 101*(2), 262–281.

Bowman-Perrott, L. D., Davis, H., Vannest, K., Williams, L., Greenwood, C. & Parker, R. (2013). Academic benefits of peer tutoring: A meta-analytic review of single-case research. *School Psychology Review, 42*(1), 39–55.

Britz, M. W., Dixon, J. & McLaughlin, T. F. (1989). The effects of peer tutoring on mathematics performance: A recent review. *British Columbia Journal of Special Education, 13*(1), 17–33.

Brooks, G. (2013). *What works for children and young people with literacy difficulties? The effectiveness of intervention schemes*. Fourth Edition. Bracknell: The Dyslexia-SpLD Trust. http://www.interventionsforliteracy.org.uk/widgets_GregBrooks/What_works_for_children_fourth_ed.pdf (retrieved 26 October 2014).

Brus, B. T. (1969). *Eén-minuut-test* [One minute test]. Nijmegen, The Netherlands: Berkhout.

Cadieux, A. & Boudreault, P. (2005). The effects of a parent–child paired reading program on reading abilities, phonological awareness and self-concept of at-risk pupils. *Reading Improvement, 42*(4), 224–237.

Cazden, C. B. (1986). Classroom discourse. In M. C. Wittrock (Ed.), *Handbook of research on teaching* (pp. 432–463). New York: Macmillan.

Cheng, Y. C. & Ku, H. Y. (2009). An investigation of the effects of reciprocal peer tutoring. *Computers in Human Behavior, 25(1)*, 40–49.

Chi, M., Siler, S., Jeong, H., Yamauchi, T. & Hausmann, R. (2001). Learning from human tutoring. *Cognitive Science, 25*, 471–533.

Chipman, M. & Roy, N. (2006). The Peer Tutoring Literacy Program™: Achieving reading fluency and developing self-esteem in elementary school students. *The ACIE Newsletter, 10*(1), 1–8.

Cohen, J. (1992). A power primer. *Psychological Bulletin, 112*, 155–159.

Cohen, P. A., Kulik, J. A. & Kulik, C. C. (1982). Educational outcomes of tutoring: A meta-analysis of findings. *American Educational Research Journal, 19(2)*, 237–248.

Cook, S., Scruggs, T., Mastropieri, M. & Casto, G. (1985). Handicapped students as tutors. *Journal of Special Education, 19*(4), 486–492.

Cortese, C. (2005). Learning through teaching. *Management Learning, 36*(1), 87–115.

Cupolillo, M., Silva, R. S., Socorro, S. & Topping, K. J. (1997). Paired reading with Brazilian first-year school failures. *Educational Psychology in Practice, 13*(2), 96–100.

DeAngelo, N. (1997). *Improving reading achievement through the use of parental involvement and paired reading*. Chicago, IL: Saint Xavier University. ERIC Accession Number ED 409 536.

Dearing, E., McCartney, K., Weiss, H. B. & Simpkins, S. (2004). The promotive effects of family education for low-income children's literacy. *Journal of School Psychology, 42*, 445–460.

De Naeghel, J., Van Keer, H., Vansteenkiste, M. & Rosseel, Y. (2012). The relation between elementary students' recreational and academic reading motivation, reading frequency, engagement, and comprehension: A self-determination theory perspective. *Journal of Educational Psychology, 104*, 1006–1021.

Dole, J. A., Nokes, J. D. & Drits, D. (2009). Cognitive strategy instruction. In G. G. Duffy & S. E. Israel (Eds), *Handbook of research on reading comprehension* (pp. 347–372). Mahwah, NJ: Lawrence Erlbaum Associates.

Duran, D. (2006). Tutoría entre iguales: Algunas prácticas. *Monográfico de la Revista Aula de Innovación Educativa, 39*(7) 153–154.

Duran, D. (2007). Llegim en parella, un programa de tutoria entre iguals, amb alumnes i famílies, per a la millora de la competència lectora. *Articles. Revista de Didàctica de la Llengua, 42*, 85–99.

Duran, D. (2014). *Aprenseñar. Evidencias e implicaciones educativas de aprender enseñando.* Madrid: Narcea.

Duran, D., Blanch, S., Corcelles, M., Fernández, M., Flores, M., Kerejeta, B., Moliner, L. & Valdebenito, V. (2011). *Bikoteka irakurtzen*. Vitoria-Gasteiz, Spain: Publicacions del Gobierno Vasco.

Duran, D., Blanch, S., Corcelles, M., Flores, M., Merino, E., Oller, M. & Utset, M. (2013). *Llegim i escrivim en parella*. Barcelona: ICE de la Universitat Autònoma de Barcelona.

Duran, D., Blanch, S., Corcelles, M., Flores, M., Oller, M. & Valdebenito, V. (2011). *Leemos en pareja, tutoría entre iguales para la competencia lectora.* Barcelona: Horsori.

Duran, D. & Flores, M. (2008). Xarxa llegim en parella, centres que treballen junts per introduir innovacions educatives. *Perspectiva Escolar, 324*, 23–31.

Duran, D. & Monereo, C. (2005). Styles and sequences of cooperative interactions in fixed and reciprocal peer tutoring. *Learning and Instruction, 15*, 179–199.

REFERENCES ■ ■ ■ ■

Duran, D. & Oller, M. (2006). La participació de les famílies en un programa de tutoria entre iguals per a la millora de la competència lectora. *Suports. Revista Catalana d'Educació Inclusiva, 10(2)*, 74–81.

Duran, D., Oller, M. & Utset, M. (2007). Nous lisons en couple: Un programme de tutelle entre pairs pour l'amélioration des compétences de lecteur. *Les Actes de Lecture. Revue de l'Association Française pour la Lecture, 97*, 17–21.

Duran, D., Torró, J. & Vilar, J. (2003). *Tutoria entre iguals, un mètode d'aprenentatge cooperatiu per a la diversitat*. Barcelona: Publicacions de l'ICE de la Universitat Autònoma de Barcelona.

Duran, D. & Utset, M. (2014). Reading in pairs network: A training model based on peer learning (pairs of teachers and school networks) for the sustainability of educational innovation. *Culture and Education, 26(2)*, 377–384.

Duran, D. & Valdebenito, V. (2014). Desarrollo de la competencia lectora a través de la tutoría entre iguales como respuesta a la diversidad del alumnado. *Revista Latinoamericana de Educación Inclusiva, 8*(2) 141–160.

Duran, D. & Vidal, V. (2004). *Tutoría entre iguales. De la teoría a la práctica*. Barcelona: Graó.

Ehri, L. C., Dreyer, L. G., Flugman, B. & Gross, A. (2007). Reading Rescue: An effective tutoring intervention model for language-minority students who are struggling readers in first grade. *American Educational Research Journal, 44*, 414–448.

Elbaum, B., Vaughn, S., Hughes, M. T. & Moody, S. W. (2000). How effective are one-on-one tutoring programs in reading for elementary students at risk for reading failure? A metaanalysis of the intervention research. *Journal of Educational Psychology, 92*(4), 605–619.

Elliott, J. A. & Hewison, J. (1994). Comprehension and interest in home reading. *British Journal of Educational Psychology, 64*, 203–220.

Ellis, M. G. (1996). *Parent–child reading programs: Involving parents in the reading intervention process*. ERIC Accession Number ED397377.

Ensergueix, P. J. & Lafont, L. (2010). Reciprocal peer tutoring in a physical education setting: Influence of peer tutor training and gender on motor performance and self-efficacy outcomes. *European Journal of Psychology of Education, 25*, 222–242.

Falchikov, N. (2001). *Learning together: Peer tutoring in higher education*. London: Routledge Falmer.

Fantuzzo, J. W., King, J. A. & Heller, L. R. (1992). Effects of reciprocal peer tutoring on mathematics and school adjustment. *Journal of Educational Psychology, 84*, 331–339.

Fantuzzo, J. W., Riggio, R. E., Connelly, S. & Dimeff, L. A. (1989). Effects of reciprocal peer tutoring on academic achievement and psychological adjustment: A component analysis. *Journal of Educational Psychology, 81*, 173–177.

Fiala, C. L. & Sheridan, S. M. (2003). Parent involvement and reading: Using curriculum-based measurement to assess the effects of Paired Reading. *Psychology in the Schools, 40*(6), 613–626.

Fitz-Gibbon, C. T. (1988). Peer tutoring as a teaching strategy. *Educational Management and Administration, 16*, 217–229.

Flores, M. & Duran, D. (2013). Effects of peer tutoring on reading self-concept. *International Journal of Educational Psychology, 2*(3), 297–324.

Flores, M. & Duran, D. (2015). Influence of a Catalan peer tutoring programme on reading comprehension and self-concept as a reader. *Journal of Research in Reading*. Published online: 18 Jan 2015, DOI: 10.1111/1467-9817.12044 (publication pending).

Fontana, D. (1990). Where do we go from here? A personal view by an educationalist. In H. C. Foot, M. J. Morgan & R. H. Shute (Eds), *Children helping children* (pp. 375–388). Chichester: John Wiley and Sons.

Frost, S. B. (1990). *Increasing reading achievement through repeated paired reading*. ERIC Accession Number ED323508.

Fuchs, D., Fuchs, L. S., Mathes, P. G. & Simmons, D. C. (1997). Peer-assisted learning strategies: Making classrooms more responsive to diversity. *American Educational Research Journal, 34*, 174–206.

Fuchs, L. S., Fuchs, D., Bentz, J, Phillips, N. B. & Hamlett, C. L. (1994). The nature of students' interactions during peer tutoring with and without prior training and experience. *American Educational Research Journal, 31,* 75–103.

Gambrell, L, B., Palmer, B. M., Codling, R. M. & Mazzoni, S. A. (1996). Assessing motivation to read. *The Reading Teacher, 49,* 518–533.

Gerber, M. M. & Kauffman, J. M. (1981). Peer tutoring in academic settings. In P. Strain (Ed.), *The utilization of classroom peers as behavior change agents* (pp.155–188). New York: Plenum.

Gilkerson, J., Richards, J. A. & Topping, K. J. (forthcoming). The impact of book reading in the early years on parent–child language interaction. *Journal for Early Childhood Literacy.*

Ginsburg-Block, M. D. & Fantuzzo, J. W. (1997). Reciprocal peer tutoring: An analysis of 'teacher' and 'student' interactions as a function of training and experience. *School Psychology Quarterly, 12,* 134–149.

Ginsburg-Block, M.D., Rohrbeck, C.A. & Fantuzzo, J.W. (2006) A meta-analytic review of social, self-concept, and behavioral outcomes of peer-assisted learning. *Journal of Educational Psychology, 98*(4), 732–749.

Glynn, T., McNaughton, S., Robinson, V. & Quinn, M. (1979). *Remedial reading at home: Helping you to help your child.* Wellington: New Zealand Council for Educational Research.

Good, T. L. & Brophy, J. E. (1997). *Looking in classrooms.* New York: Addison Wesley Longman.

Graesser, A. C., D'Mello, S. & Cade, W. (2011). Instruction based on tutoring. In R. E. Mayer and P. A. Alexander (Eds), *Handbook of research on learning and instruction* (pp. 408–426). New York: Taylor & Francis.

Graesser, A. C. & McNamara, D. (2010). Self-regulated learning in learning environments with pedagogical agents that interact in natural language. *Educational Psychologist, 45,* 234–244.

Graesser, A. C. & Person, N. (1994). Question asking during tutoring. *American Educational Research Journal, 31,* 104–137.

Graesser, A. C. Person, N. & Magliano, J. (1995). Collaborative dialogue patterns in naturalistic one-to-one tutoring. *Applied Cognitive Psychology, 9,* 495–522.

Greenwood, C. R., Carta, J. C. & Hall, R. V. (1988). The use of peer tutoring strategies in classroom management and educational instruction. *School Psychology Review, 17,* 258–275.

Greenwood, C. R., Carta, J. & Kamps, D. (1990). Teacher mediated versus peer-mediated instruction: A review of advantages and disadvantages. In H. C. Foot, M. J. Morgan & R. H. Shute (Eds), *Children helping children.* Chichester: John Wiley and Sons.

Greenwood, C. R. & Delquadri, J. C. (1995). Classwide peer tutoring and the prevention of school failure. *Preventing School Failure, 39,* 21–25.

Griffin, M. M. & Griffin, B. W. (1998). An investigation of the effect of reciprocal peer tutoring on achievement, self-efficacy, and test anxiety. *Contemporary Educational Psychology, 23,* 298–311.

Guthrie, J. T. (2003). Concept-oriented reading instruction. In A. P. Sweet & C. E. Snow (Eds), *Rethinking reading comprehension* (pp. 115–140). New York: The Guilford Press.

Guthrie, J. T. & Cox, K. E. (2001). Classroom conditions for motivation and engagement in reading. *Educational Psychology Review, 13,* 283–302.

Hadwin, A. F., Wozney, L. & Pontin, O. (2005). Scaffolding the appropriation of self-regulatory activity: A socio-cultural analysis of changes in teacher-student discourse about a graduate research portfolio. *Instructional Science, 33,* 413–450.

Hannon, P. (1987). A study of the effects of parental involvement in the teaching of reading on children's reading test performance. *British Journal of Educational Psychology, 57*(1), 56–72.

Hartman, H. J. (2001). Developing students' metacognitive knowledge and skills. In H. J. Hartman (Ed.), *Metacognition in learning and instruction* (pp. 33–68). Dordrecht, The Netherlands: Kluwer Academic Publishers.

Hattie, J. (2006). Cross-age tutoring and the Reading Together program. *Studies in Educational Evaluation, 32*(2), 100–124.

Henk, W. A. & Melnick, S. A. (1995). The Reader Self-Perception Scale: A new tool for measuring how children feel about themselves as readers. *The Reading Teacher, 48*(6), 470–482.

REFERENCES ▪ ▪ ▪ ▪

Hewison, J. & Tizard, J. (1980). Parental involvement and reading attainment. *British Journal of Educational Psychology, 50,* 209–215.

Huemer, S., Landerl, K., Aro, M. & Lyytinen, H. (2008). Training reading fluency among poor readers of German: Many ways to the goal. *Annals of Dyslexia, 58*(2), 115–137.

Jacobs, J. E. & Paris, S. G. (1987). Children's metacognition about reading: Issues in definition, measurement, and instruction. *Educational Psychologist, 22,* 255–278.

Jiménez, J. & O'Shanahan, I. (2008). Enseñanza de la lectura: De la teoría y la investigación a la práctica educativa. *Revista Iberoamericana de Educación, 44(5),* 6–19.

Johnson, D. & Johnson, R. (2009). An educational psychology success story: Social interdependence theory and cooperative learning. *Educational Researcher, 38(5),* 365–379.

Juel, C. (1996). What makes literacy tutoring effective? *Reading Research Quarterly, 31,* 268–289.

Jun, S. W., Ramirez, G. & Cumming, A. (2010). Tutoring adolescents in literacy: A meta-analysis. *Journal of Education, 45(2),* 219–238.

Kagan, S. (2005). New cooperative learning, multiple intelligences and inclusion. In J. W. Putnam (Ed.), *Cooperative learning and strategies for inclusion* (pp. 105–136). Baltimore, MA: Paul H. Brookes Publishing.

Kartch, D., Marks, C. & Reitz, M. (1999). *Examining reading fluency in primary children.* ERIC Accession Number ED435973.

King, A. (1998). Transactive peer tutoring: Distributing cognition and metacognition. *Educational Psychology Review, 10,* 57–74.

King, A., Staffieri, A. & Adelgais, A. (1998). Mutual peer tutoring: Effect of structuring tutorial interaction to scaffold peer learning. *Journal of Educational Psychology, 90,* 134–152.

King-Sears, M. E. & Bradley, D. F. (1995). Classwide peer tutoring. *Preventing School Failure, 40,* 29–36.

Klingner, J. K. & Vaughn, S. (1996). Reciprocal teaching of reading comprehension strategies for students with learning disabilities who use English as a second language. *The Elementary School Journal, 96,* 275–293.

Lam, J. W. I., Cheung, W. M. & Lam, R. Y. H. (2009). Learning to read: The reading performance of Hong Kong primary students compared with that in developed countries around the world in PIRLS 2001 and 2006. *Chinese Education and Society, 42* (3), 6–32.

Lam, S., Chow-Yeung, K., Wong, B. P. H., Lau, K. K. & Tse, S. I. (2013). Involving parents in Paired Reading with preschoolers: Results from a randomized controlled trial. *Contemporary Educational Psychology, 38*(2), 126–135.

Law, M. & Kratochwill, T. R. (1993) Paired Reading: An evaluation of a parent tutorial program. *School Psychology International, 14,* 119–147.

Leach, C. (1993). *The effect of a Paired Reading program on reading achievement and attitude in a third grade classroom.* Wayne, NJ: William Paterson College. ERIC Accession Number 358424.

Leung, K. C. (2014). Preliminary empirical model of crucial determinants of best practice for peer tutoring on academic achievement. *Journal of Educational Psychology.* Advance online publication: http://dx.doi.org/10.1037/a0037698.

Leung, K. C., Marsh, H. W. & Craven, R. G. (2005). *Are peer tutoring programs effective in promoting academic achievement and self-concept in educational settings? A meta-analytical review.* Association for Active Educational Researchers Annual Conference, Cairns, Australia. Paper LEU05421. http://www.aare.edu.au/05pap/abs05.htm#L (retrieved 23 February 2009).

Li, D. & Nes, S. (2001). Using Paired Reading to help ESL students become fluent and accurate readers. *Reading Improvement, 38*(2), 50–61.

Loke, A. & Chow, F. (2007). Learning partnership. The experience of peer tutoring among nursing students: A qualitative study. *International Journal of Nursing Studies, 44,* 237–244.

Maher, C., Maher, B. & Thurston, C. (1998). Disruptive students as tutors: A systems approach to planning and evaluation of programs. In K. J. Topping & S. Ehly (Eds), *Peer-assisted learning* (pp. 145–163). Mahwah, NJ: Lawrence Erlbaum Associates.

Martínez, R. A. (1992). La participación de los padres en el centro escolar: Una forma de intervención comunitaria sobre las dificultades escolares. *Bordón, 44*(2), 171–175.

Martínez, R. A. (2004). Fomento de las relaciones de colaboración entre las familias y el profesorado. *Infancia y aprendizaje, 27*(4), 425–435.

Mathes, P. G. & Fuchs, L. S. (1994). The efficacy of peer tutoring in reading for students with mild disabilities: A best-evidence synthesis. *School Psychology Review, 23(1),* 59–80.

McKenna, M. C. & Kear, D. J. (1990). Measuring attitude toward reading: A new tool for teachers. *The Reading Teacher, 43*(9), 626–639.

McKenna, M. C., Kear, D. J. & Ellsworth, R. A. (1995). Children's attitudes toward reading: A national survey. *Reading Research Quarterly, 30*(4), 934–956.

McLuckie, J. & Topping, K. J. (2004). Transferable skills for online peer learning. *Assessment and Evaluation in Higher Education, 29,* 563–584.

Mercer, N. (1996). The quality of talk in children's collaborative activity in the classroom. *Learning and Instruction, 6,* 359–377.

Miller, B. V. & Kratochwill, T. R. (1996). An evaluation of the Paired Reading program using competency-based training. *School Psychology International, 17,* 269–291.

Miller, D., Topping, K. J. & Thurston, A. (2010). Peer tutoring in reading: The effects of role and organization on two dimensions of self-esteem. *British Journal of Educational Psychology, 80(3),* 417–433.

Monteiro, V. (2013). Promoting reading motivation by reading together. *Reading Psychology, 34*(4), 301–335.

Muldowney, C. J. (1995). *The effect of a Paired Reading program on reading achievement in a first grade classroom.* ERIC Accession Number ED379634.

Mullis, I. V. S., Martin, M. O., Foy, P. & Drucker, K. T. (2012). *The PIRLS 2011 international results in reading.* Chestnut Hill, MA: TIMSS & PIRLS International Study Center, Boston College.

Murad, C. R. & Topping, K. J. (2000). Parents as reading tutors for first graders in Brazil. *School Psychology International, 21*(2), 152–171.

Nailing, X. (2010). *Family factors and student outcomes.* Santa Mónica, CA: RAND Corporation. http://www.rand.org/content/dam/rand/pubs/rgs_dissertations/2010/RAND_RGSD256.pdf (retrieved 4 November 2014).

National Institute of Child Health and Human Development (2000). *Report of the National Reading Panel. Teaching children to read: An evidence-based assessment of the scientific research literature on reading and its implications for reading instruction* (NIH Publication No. 00-4769). Washington, DC: US Government Printing Office. (Teacher's Guide at http://www.nichd.nih.gov/publications/pubs/prf_k-3/Documents/PRFbooklet.pdf.)

Netten, A., Droop, M. & Verhoeven, L. (2011). Predictors of reading literacy for first and second language learners. *Reading and Writing: An Interdisciplinary Journal, 24,* 413–425.

Oddo, M., Barnett, D. W., Hawkins, R. O. & Musti-Rao, S. (2010). Reciprocal peer tutoring and repeated reading: Increasing practicality using student groups. *Psychology in the Schools, 47,* 842–858.

Organisation for Economic Cooperation and Development (OECD) (2004). *Learning for tomorrow's world. First results from PISA 2003.* Paris: OECD.

OECD (2009). *Assessment framework. Key competencies in reading, mathematics and science.* Paris: OECD. http://www.oecd.org/dataoecd/11/40/44455820.pdf (retrieved 4 November 2014).

OECD (2014). *PISA 2012 results: What students know and can do: student performance in mathematics, reading and science* (Volume I, revised edition, February 2014). Paris: OECD. http://www.oecd.org/pisa/keyfindings/pisa-2012-results-volume-I.pdf (retrieved 4 November 2014).

Ofsted (2001). *Family learning: A survey of good practice.* London: HMSO.

Okilwa, N. S. A. & Shelby, L. (2010). The effects of peer tutoring on academic performance of students with disabilities in grades 6 through 12: A synthesis of the literature. *Remedial and Special Education, 31,* 450–463.

REFERENCES ■ ■ ■ ■

Oliva, A. & Palacios, J. (1998). Familia y escuela: Padres profesores. In M. J. Rodrigo & J. Palacios (Eds), *Familia y desarrollo humano* (pp. 333–352). Madrid: Alianza Editorial.

Osguthorpe, R. T. & Scruggs, T. E. (1986). Special education students as tutors: A review and analysis. *RASE: Remedial & Special Education, 7*(4), 15–25.

Osguthorpe, R. T. & Scruggs, T. E. (1990). Special education students as tutors: A review and analysis. In S. Goodlad & B. Hirst (Eds), *Explorations in peer tutoring* (pp. 176–193). Oxford: Blackwell.

Overett, J. & Donald, D. (1998). Paired Reading: Effects of a parent involvement programme in a disadvantaged community in South Africa. *British Journal of Educational Psychology, 68*, 347–356.

Pakulski, L. A. & Kaderavek, J. N. (2012). Reading intervention to improve narrative production, narrative comprehension, and motivation and interest of children with hearing loss. *Volta Review, 112*(2), 87–112.

Parr, J. M. & Townsend, M. A. R. (2002). Environments, processes, and mechanisms in peer learning. *International Journal of Educational Research, 37*, 403–423.

Pereira-Laird, J. A. & Deane, F. P. (1997). Development and validation of a self-report measure of reading strategy use. *Reading Psychology, 18*, 185–235.

Person, N. K. & Graesser, A. C. (1999). Evolution of discourse during cross-age tutoring. In A. M. O'Donnell & A. King (Eds), *Cognitive perspectives on peer learning* (pp. 69–86). Mahwah, NJ: Lawrence Erlbaum Associates.

Piaget, J. (1977). *The development of thought: Equilibration of cognitive structures*. New York: Viking.

Ploetzner, R., Dillenbourg, P., Preier, M. & Traum, D. (1999). Learning by explaining to oneself and to others. In P. Dillenbourg (Ed.), *Collaborative learning: Cognitive and computational approaches* (pp. 103–121). New York: Elsevier Science Publishers.

Powell, D. R., Son, S. H., File, N. & San Juan, R. R. (2010). Parent-school relationships and children's academic and social outcomes in public school pre-kindergarten. *Journal of School Psychology, 48*, 269–292.

Prescott-Griffin, M. L. (2005). *Reader to reader: Building independence through peer partnerships*. Portsmouth, NH: Heinemann.

Pressley, M. & Harris, K. R. (2006). Cognitive strategies instruction: From basic research to classroom instruction. In P. A. Alexander & P. H. Wine (Eds), *Handbook of educational psychology* (pp. 265–286). Mahwah, NJ: Lawrence Erlbaum Associates

Ritchen, D. & Salvanik, L. (2003). *Key competencies for a successful life and a well-functioning society*. Göttingen: Hogrefe & Huber Publishers.

Ritter, G. W., Barnett, J. H., Denny, G. S. & Albin, G. R. (2009). The effectiveness of volunteer tutoring programs for elementary and middle school students: A meta-analysis. *Review of Educational Research, 79*(1), 3–31.

Robinson, D. R., Schofield, J. W. & Steers-Wentzell, K. L. (2005). Peer and cross-age tutoring in math: Outcomes and their design implications. *Educational Psychology Review, 17*(4), 327–362.

Rohrbeck, C. A., Ginsburg-Block, M. D., Fantuzzo, J. W. & Miller, T. R. (2003). Peer-assisted learning interventions with elementary school students: A meta-analytic review. *Journal of Educational Psychology, 95*(2), 240–257.

Roller, C. M. (1998). *So . . . what's tutor to do?* Newark, DE: International Reading Association.

Roscoe, R. D. (2014). Self-monitoring and knowledge building in learning by teaching. *Instructional Science, 42*, 327–351.

Roscoe, R. D. & Chi, M. (2007). Understanding tutor learning; Knowledge-building and knowledge-telling in peer tutors' explanations and questions. *Review of Educational Research, 77(4)*, 334–374.

Roscoe, R. D. & Chi, M. (2008). Tutor learning: The role of explaining and responding to questions. *Instructional Science, 36*, 321–350.

Rué, J. (1998). El aula: Un espacio para la cooperación. In C. Mir (Ed.), *Cooperar en la escuela. La responsabilidad de educar para la democracia* (pp. 17–49). Barcelona: Editorial Graó.

Ryan, J., Reid, R. & Epstein, M. H. (2004). Peer-mediated intervention studies on academic achievement for students with EBD: A review. *Remedial and Special Education, 25*(6), 330–347.

Rychen, D. S. & Salganik, L. H. (Eds) (2001). *Defining and selecting key competences.* Göttlngen: Hogrefe & Huber.

Samway, K. D., Whang, G. & Pippit, M. (1995) *Buddy reading: Cross-age tutoring in a multicultural school.* Portsmouth, NH: Heinemann.

Schraw, G., Crippen, K. J. & Hartley K. (2006). Promoting self-regulation in science education: Metacognition as part of a broader perspective on learning. *Research in Science Education, 36,* 111–139.

Scoble, J., Topping, K. J. & Wigglesworth, C. (1988). Training family and friends as adult literacy tutors. *Journal of Reading (Journal of Adolescent and Adult Literacy), 31*(5), 410–417 (also in: Radencich, M. C. (Ed.) (1994), *Adult literacy.* Newark DE: International Reading Association).

Scruggs, T. E. & Mastropieri, M. A. (1998). Tutoring and students with special needs. In K. J. Topping & S. Ehly (Eds), *Peer-assisted learning* (pp. 165–182). Mahwah, NJ: Lawrence Erlbaum Associates.

Seymour, P. H. K. (2005). Early reading development in European orthographies. In M. J. Snowling & C. Hulme (Eds), *The science of reading: A handbook* (pp. 296–315). Oxford: Blackwell.

Shah-Wundenberg, M., Wyse, D. & Chaplain, R. (2013). Parents helping their children learn to read: The effectiveness of Paired Reading and hearing reading in a developing country context. *Journal of Early Childhood Literacy, 13*(4), 471–500.

Shamir, A. & Lazerovitz, T. (2007). Peer mediation intervention for scaffolding self-regulated learning among children with learning disabilities. *European Journal of Special Needs Education, 22*(3), 255–273.

Shamir, A. & Tzuriel, D. (2004). Children's meditational teaching style as a function of intervention for cross-age peer mediation. *School Psychology International, 25,* 59–78.

Shamir, A., Zion, M. & Spector-Levi, O. (2008). Peer tutoring, metacognitive processes and multimedia problem-based learning: The effect of mediation training on critical thinking. *Journal of Science Education and Technology, 17,* 384–398.

Sharan, S. & Sharan, Y. (1994). *Handbook of cooperative learning methods.* London: Praeger.

Sharan, Y. (2010). Cooperative learning for academic and social gains: Valued pedagogy, problematic practice. *European Journal of Education, 45*(2), 300–313.

Sharp, S. R. & Skinner, C. H. (2004). Using interdependent group contingencies with randomly selected criteria and Paired Reading to enhance class-wide reading performance. *Journal of Applied School Psychology, 20*(2), 29–45.

Shegar, C. (2009). Buddy reading in a Singaporean primary school: Implications for training and research. *RELC Journal, 40*(2), 133–148.

Sideridis, G., Utley, C., Greenwood, C., Delquadri, J., Dawson, H., Palmer, P. & Reddy, S. (1997). Classwide peer tutoring: Effects on the spelling performance and social interactions of students with mild disabilities and their typical peers in an integrated instructional setting. *Journal of Behavioral Education, 7*(4), 435–462.

Simmons, D. C., Fuchs, L. S., Fuchs, D., Mathes, P. G. & Hodge, J. P. (1995). Effects of explicit teaching and peer tutoring on the reading achievement of learning-disabled and low-performing students in regular classrooms. *The Elementary School Journal, 95,* 387–408.

Snow, C. E. & Sweet, A. P. (2003). Reading for comprehension. In A. P. Sweet & C. E. Snow (Eds), *Rethinking reading comprehension* (pp. 1–11). New York: The Guilford Press.

Solé, I. (1992). *Estrategias de lectura.* Barcelona: Graó.

Solé, I. (2005). PISA, la lectura y sus lecturas. *Aula de Innovación Educativa, 139,* 22–27.

Spencer, V.G. (2006). Peer tutoring and students with emotional or behavioral disorders: A review of the literature. *Behavioral Disorders, 2*(31), 204–222.

REFERENCES ▪ ▪ ▪ ▪

Spencer, V. G. & Balboni, G. (2003). Can students with mental retardation teach their peers? *Education and Training in Mental Retardation and Developmental Disabilities, 38*(1), 32–61.

Staphorsius, G. & Krom, R. (1996). *Toetsen begrijpend lezen* [Reading comprehension tests]. Arnhem, The Netherlands: Cito.

Toomey, D. (1991). *Parents hearing reading: Lessons for school practice from the British and Australasian research.* Paper presented at the 72nd Annual Meeting of the American Educational Research Association (3–7 April, Chicago, IL). ERIC Accession Number ED 333355.

Toomey, D. (1993). Parents hearing their children read: A review. *Educational Research, 35*(3), 223–36.

Topping, K. J. (1992a). Short- and long-term follow-up of parental involvement in reading projects. *British Educational Research Journal, 18*(4), 369–379.

Topping, K. J. (1992b). The effectiveness of paired reading in ethnic minority homes. *Multicultural Teaching, 10*(2), 19–23.

Topping, K. J. (1995). *Paired reading, spelling and writing: The handbook for teachers and parents.* London and New York: Cassell.

Topping, K. J. (1996). Effective peer tutoring in further and higher education: A typology and review of the literature. *Higher Education, 32*, 321–345.

Topping, K. J. (1997) Process and outcome in paired reading: A reply to Winter. *Educational Psychology in Practice, 13*(2), 75–86.

Topping, K. J. (2000). *Tutoring.* Geneva: International Academy of Education.

Topping, K. J. (2001a). *Thinking reading writing. A practical guide to paired learning with peers, parents and volunteers.* London: Continuum.

Topping, K. J. (2001b). *Peer assisted learning. A practical guide for teachers.* Cambridge, MA: Brookline Books.

Topping, K. J. (2005). Trends in peer learning. *Educational Psychology, 25*, 631–645.

Topping, K. J. (2006). *Scotland reads: Volunteer training programme and pack.* Edinburgh: Project Scotland.

Topping, K. J., & Bamford, J. (1998). *Parental involvement and peer tutoring in mathematics and science: Developing paired maths and paired science.* London: Fulton.

Topping, K. J. & Bryce, A. (2004). Cross-age peer tutoring of reading and thinking: Influence on thinking skills. *Educational Psychology, 24*, 595–621.

Topping, K. J., Campbell, J., Douglas, W. & Smith, A. (2003). Cross-age peer tutoring in mathematics with seven- and eleven-year olds: Influence on mathematical vocabulary, strategic dialogue and self-concept. *Educational Research, 45*, 287–308.

Topping, K. J. & Ehly, S. (1998). *Peer-assisted learning.* Mahwah, NJ: Lawrence Erlbaum Associates.

Topping, K. J. & Ehly, S. (2001). Peer assisted learning: A framework for consultation. *Journal of Educational and Psychological Consultation, 12*, 113–132.

Topping, K. J. & Hogan, J. (1999). *Read on: Paired reading and thinking video resource pack.* London: BP Educational Services.

Topping, K. J. & Lindsay, G. A. (1992a). Paired Reading: A review of the literature. *Research Papers in Education, 7*(3), 199–246.

Topping, K. J. & Lindsay, G. A. (1992b). Parental involvement in reading: The influence of socio-economic status and supportive home visiting. *Children and Society, 5*(4), 306–316.

Topping, K. J., Miller, D., Thurston, A., McGavock, K. & Conlin, N. (2011). Peer tutoring in reading in Scotland: Thinking big. *Literacy, 45*(1), 3–9.

Topping, K. J., Thurston, A., McGavock, K. & Conlin, N. (2012). Outcomes and process in reading tutoring. *Educational Research, 54*(3), 239–258.

Topping, K. J. & Whiteley, M. (1990). Participant evaluation of parent-tutored and peer-tutored projects in reading. *Educational Research, 32*(1), 14–32.

Topping, K. J. & Whiteley, M. (1993). Sex differences in the effectiveness of peer tutoring. *School Psychology International, 14*(1), 57–67.

Tymms, P., Merrell, C., Andor, J., Topping, K. J. & Thurston, A. (2011). Improving attainment across a whole district: Peer tutoring in a randomised controlled trial. *School Effectiveness and School Improvement, 22*(3), 265–289.

Utley, C. A. & Mortweet, S. L. (1997). Peer-mediated instruction and interventions. *Focus on Exceptional Children, 29,* 69–92.

Vaessen, K., Walraven, G. & van Wissen, M. (1998). *Tutoring en mentoring. Een klassieke methode in een moderne context.* [Tutoring and mentoring. A classical method in a modern context.] Utrecht: Sardes.

Valdebenito, V. & Duran, D. (2010). Implicación familiar en un programa de tutoría entre iguales para la mejora de la comprensión y la velocidad lectora. In J. J. Gázquez Linares & M. C. Pérez Fuentes (Eds), *Investigación en convivencia familiar. Variables relacionadas* (pp. 433–438). Granada: Editorial GEU.

Valdebenito, V. & Duran, D. (2013). La tutoría entre iguales como un potente recurso de aprendizaje entre alumnos: Efectos, fluidez y comprensión lectora. *Perspectiva Educacional, 52(*2), 154–176.

Van den Broek, P. & Kremer, K. E. (2000). The mind in action: What it means to comprehend during reading. In B. M. Taylor, M. F. Graves & P. Van den Broek (Eds), *Reading for meaning. Fostering comprehension in the middle grades* (pp. 1–13). New York: Teachers College Press.

Van Keer, H. (2002). *Een Boek voor Twee. Strategieën voor begrijpend lezen via peer tutoring.* [A Book for Two. Strategies for reading comprehension by means of peer tutoring.] Antwerpen: Garant.

Van Keer, H. (2004). Fostering reading comprehension in fifth grade by explicit instruction in reading strategies and peer tutoring. *British Journal of Educational Psychology, 74*(1), 37–70.

Van Keer, H. & Vanderlinde, R. (2008). *Nog een Boek voor Twee. Strategieën voor begrijpend lezen via peer tutoring.* [Another Book for Two. Strategies for reading comprehension by means of peer tutoring.] Antwerpen: Garant.

Van Keer, H. & Vanderlinde, R. (2010). The impact of cross-age peer tutoring on third and sixth graders' reading strategy awareness, reading strategy use and reading comprehension. *Middle Grades Research Journal, 5,* 33–46.

Van Keer, H. & Vanderlinde, R. (2013). A book for two! Peer tutoring and reading comprehension in elementary school practice. *Phi Delta Kappan, 94,* 54–58.

Van Keer, H. & Verhaeghe, J. P. (2005a). Effects of explicit reading strategies instruction and peer tutoring in second and fifth graders' reading comprehension and self-efficacy perceptions. *Journal of Experimental Education, 73,* 291–329.

Van Keer, H. & Verhaeghe, J. P. (2005b). Comparing two teacher training programs for innovating reading comprehension instruction with regard to teachers' experiences and student outcomes. *Teaching and Teacher Education, 21,* 543–562.

VanLehn, K. (2011). The relative effectiveness of human tutoring, intelligent tutoring systems, and other tutoring systems. *Educational Psychologist, 46,* 197–221.

VanLehn, K., Graesser, A. C., Jackson, G. T., Jordan, P., Olney, A. & Rosé, C. P. (2007). When are tutorial dialogues more effective than reading? *Cognitive Science, 31,* 3–62.

Van Meter, P. & Stevens, R. J. (2000). The role of theory in the study of peer collaboration. *Journal of Experimental Education, 69,* 113–127.

Vaughn, S. & Linan-Thompson, S. (2004). *Research-based methods for reading instruction. Grades K–3.* Alexandria, VA: Association for Supervision and Curriculum Development.

Vellutino, F. R. (2003). Individual differences as sources of variability in reading comprehension in elementary school children. In A. P. Sweet & C. E . Snow (Eds), *Rethinking reading comprehension* (pp. 51–81). New York: The Guilford Press.

Verhoeven, L. (1993). *Lezen met begrip 1* [Reading with comprehension 1]. Arnhem, The Netherlands: Cito.

Vilà, M. (2002). Hablar para aprender a hablar mejor: El equilibrio entre el uso de la lengua y la reflexión. *Aula de Innovación Educativa, 11,* 18–22.

REFERENCES ■ ■ ■ ■

Volet, S., Vauras, M. & Salonen, P. (2009). Self- and social regulation in learning contexts: An integrative perspective. *Educational Psychologist, 44*, 215–226.

Vygotsky, L. S. (1978). *Mind in society: The development of higher psychological processes.* Cambridge, MA: Harvard University Press.

Walberg, H. & Paik, S. (2000). *Effective educational practices.* Geneva: International Academy of Education.

Warrington, M. J. & George, P. (2014). Reading for pleasure in paradise: Paired Reading in Antigua and Barbuda. *Literacy, 48*(2), 66–71.

Wasik, B. (1997). *Volunteer tutoring programs. A review of research on achievement outcomes.* Baltimore, MA: Center for Research of the Education of Students Placed at Risk.

Webb, N. M., Ing, M., Kersting, N. & Nemer, K. M. (2006). Help seeking in cooperative learning groups. In S. A. Karabenick & R. S. Newman (Eds). *Help seeking in academic settings. Goals, groups, and context* (pp. 45–88). Mahwah, NJ: Lawrence Erlbaum Associates.

Webb, N. M. & Mastergeorge, A. (2003). Promoting effective helping behaviour in peer-directed groups. *International Journal of Educational Research, 39*, 73–97.

Wells, G. (1999). *Dialogic inquiry.* Cambridge: The Press Syndicate of the University of Cambridge.

Wheldall, K. & Colmar, S. (1990). Peer tutoring in low-progress readers using Pause, Prompt and Praise. In H. Foot, M. Morgan & R. Shute (Eds). *Children helping children* (pp. 117–134). Chichester: John Willey and Sons.

Winter, S. (1996) Paired Reading: Three questions. *Educational Psychology in Practice, 12*(3), 33–41.

Wolfendale, S. & Topping, K. J. (Eds) (1996). *Family involvement in literacy: Effective partnerships in education.* London: Cassell.

Ziegler, J. & Goswami, U. (2005). Reading acquisition, developmental dyslexia, and skilled reading across languages: A psycholinguistic grain size theory. *Psychological Bulletin, 131*(1), 3–29.

NOTE

The Paired Reading and Paired Learning bulletins are available internationally from the Educational Resources Information Center (ERIC) (reference numbers: 1985—ED2285124; 1986—ED285125; 1987—ED285126; 1988—ED298429; 1989—ED313656).

INDEX